"*Gaze Into the Abyss* offers new and valuable insights into Morrison's writing. Jim's poetic gift was often ignored and certainly not fully appreciated while he lived and I, for one, am grateful for this in-depth look."

James Riordan, author of *Break on Through: The Life and Death of Jim Morrison.*

"No other rock poet went so deep into his soul. That is what separates Jim Morrison from the rest. Jim and his words were timeless and reached deep into those people who got it, turning them into worshippers. Even the new generations get it. This book by William Cook finally addresses the phenomenon that was Jim Morrison the poet."

Paul Ferrara, Director, Author & Photographer of The Doors & friend of Jim Morrison.

"William Cook has written an admirable analysis of Jim Morrison's poetry, taking us beyond the sophomoric judgements of most music journalists and critics. Anyone who seeks a deeper understanding of Morrison as a poet will find Cook's work an important addition to what might be called the growing field of Doors studies."

David Shiang, author of *Jim Morrison and the Secret Gold Mine: Breaking through the Doors to Hidden Reality and the Mind of God,*

GAZE INTO THE ABYSS

The Poetry of Jim Morrison

WILLIAM COOK

GAZE INTO THE ABYSS:
THE POETRY OF JIM MORRISON
by William Cook
2nd Edition
[1. Literary Criticism. 2. Musical Biography]

Copyright © 2020, William Cook.
Published by Unboxed Brain Books.

Poetry of Jim Morrison © 1985, 1990, 1991 by the Estate of James
Douglas Morrison.

All rights reserved under International and Pan-American Copyright
Conventions. Except for brief quotations for review purposes, no part
of this book may be reproduced in any form without the permission
of Unboxed Brain Books and/or the author.

Book cover design & illustrations © by William Cook
All photographic images are in the public domain at time of
publication.

Previously published in abridged form by New Street
Communications, LLC (2015)

*For my beautiful wife.
Without her support,
none of this would be possible.*

Thanks also to Jim Cherry.

CLARK COUNTY SHERIFF DEPT. LAS VEGAS, NEVADA	MORRISON	JIM	DOUGLAS	132938
Signature of Person Fingerprinted	Last Name	First Name	Middle Name	Number
	Race	Sex	FPC:	
	W	M	30 W 7	
Signature of Official Taking Prints	Date of Birth	Place of Birth	20 W R	
	12-8-43	Fla.		
Date Fingerprinted	Height	Weight	REF:	
1-29-68	5'11	145		
Classed	Hair	Eyes		
Filed	BRN	HZL		

Contents

Foreword by Jim Cherry	xv
Preface	xix
Introduction	xxi
I. Critiquing the Myth of Morrison	1
II. Motivation & Motif	8
III. Philosophy, Poetry, & America	22
IV. Poetic & Poet	36
V. Shamanism, Ideals, & Ritual	54
VI. The Influence of Style	67
VII. Conclusions	79
Appendix	89
Bibliography	95
Plea to the Reader	101
About the Author	103
Also by William Cook	105

Foreword by Jim Cherry

Jim Morrison was a trickster. He lured us in with apocryphal songs that captured the popular audiences' imagination, then he sprang his poetry on us and we were hooked! We would have followed him anywhere, but he didn't want followers. He wanted to show us what he saw: a wild world of mystery, of wicked dangers, of pristine landscapes, wildernesses in which we could create new worlds which could be "limitless and free," instead of following the old rules, the old ideas, the old dogmas. Morrison's way to show us these new worlds was with sensuous poetry.

Jim Morrison implored us to break the "mind forged manacles" that we've imprisoned our thinking with and that's exactly what William Cook wants you to do in *Gaze into the Abyss: The Poetry of Jim Morrison*. Forget Jim Morrison the rock star, the sex symbol, the singer; forget anything you think you know about Jim Morrison and see the poet and the poetry.

Today, poetry is no longer a popular source of

transmitting ideas; instead, poetry is a language we seem to have forgotten. Poetry is the painting of the written word, where words are thick with meaning and sometimes difficult to deal with. And so too is the subject matter of Morrison's poetry with all its confrontational complexity. He could have easily written about peace, love, flowers, even revolution; instead he chose more complex ideas. Morrison was wrestling with the gods and demons of existence, the conscious and the unconscious, dream and reality, the mysteries of ourselves and our place in this world and, perhaps, in the next.

Cook rightly makes the connection between alchemy, shamanism and Nietzsche; all are attempts to break down life and experience to its purest form. In search of this purity, Morrison imbues his words with meaning and resonance.

Early on, ancient shamanic seers used the power of words to invoke the spirit world with chants, prayers, poems, and songs. That's what Jim Morrison gave us: invocations, prayers, poems and songs that hold seemingly great, but obscure, significance.

The words tantalise us with meaning that seems just out of reach and Cook gives us some of the keys which we can use to understand, interpret and open the doors to Jim Morrison's poetry.

In your eagerness for understanding Morrison's poetry, when you read *Gaze into the Abyss: The Poetry of Jim Morrison*, you may be tempted to consume it, but DON'T. Read it a section at a time and at your own pace. Consider what Cook has pointed out; ruminate, ponder, think about it and when you're finished, read

Jim Morrison's poetry and see what new worlds open up before your eyes.

> Jim Cherry, author of *The Doors Examined*, *The Last Stage*, and *The Captured Dead*

Preface

This new edition of *Gaze Into The Abyss: The Poetry of Jim Morrison* has been updated to reflect new understanding of Morrison and his poetic. I had the good fortune to correspond with a good friend of Jim's who was part of his inner-sanctum and a confidante of Morrison's. They discussed literature and art on many occasions, the conversations of which prove insightful in terms of understanding and interpreting the aesthetic and philosophical underpinnings of Morrison's poetry. The insights shared with me in confidence have tempered my review of this edition and honed my earlier critique to what is, hopefully, a much more accurate portrayal of the influences and meaning behind Morrison's poetry.

My own understanding of Morrison's poems has grown with maturity and it is still pleases me that my earlier judgements about the strength of his poetry still stand today. If anything, Morrison's ability as a poet is more widely recognized now with a number of other serious critiques (mainly in the form of academic theses) freely available to read online. His popularity doesn't seem to have wavered in terms of his long-standing appeal as a sex symbol and performer, and it is heartening to see that sales of his poetry books have continued to rank well. It is my hope that this short volume will add to the growing awareness of Jim Morrison's poetry and the mystical but humanistic world-view that can be found in his work. His poetry was not the mere meanderings of a drug and booze-addled pop-star, as you will discover in *Gaze Into The Abyss* the depth of meaning and the profundity of his philosophical musings give the verse a legitimacy that can no longer be ignored.

William Cook, 2020.

Introduction

'If we affirm one single moment, we thus affirm not only ourselves but all existence. For nothing is self-sufficient, neither in us ourselves nor in things; and if our soul has trembled with happiness and sounded like a harp string just once, all eternity was needed to produce this one event—and in this single moment of affirmation all eternity was called good, redeemed, justified, and affirmed.'

Nietzsche, Friedrich, *The Will to Power*

James Douglas Morrison's poetry was born out of a period of tumultuous social and political change in American and world history. Aside from his cultural, philosophical and political perspectives, Morrison's verse speaks with an understanding of the world of literature, especially of the traditions that shaped the poetry of his age. His poetry also expresses his own experiences, thoughts, development, and maturation as a poet — from his musings on film at UCLA in *The*

Lords and The New Creatures, to his final poems in *Wilderness* and *The American Night*.[1] Despite his critics and detractors, it is my contention that Morrison *is* an important American poet, whose work is worthy of serious consideration in relation to its place in the American literary tradition.

By discussing the poetry in terms of the quality and significance of the work, Morrison is revealed to be a proficient and interesting American poet who deserves recognition. In order to validate my claim that he is a significant poet worthy of canonical consideration, the focus of this critique will be on Morrison's own words and poetry. Special consideration is given to his early work and the influence of cultural, philosophical and literary narratives and ideas.

The examination of these influences, which usually present themselves in Morrison's work in both a deliberate and oblique fashion, reveals his poetry to be of a character more complex than most critical appraisals would suggest. Morrison shows in his verse the ability to alter and transform ideas and text in order to lift narrative above mere derivative imitation. This transformative ability and focus, which characterises the greater body of his work, gives his poetry an interesting dimension that is charged with imperative and meaning.

Morrison's poetry is characterised by an ambiguity of meaning and allusion that serves to express subconscious thought, archetypal myth and the chaos of experience. His ability to employ this trope throughout most of his poetry effectively creates a profound signature style, especially when combined with the usage of evocative symbolism and language, which is of both contemporary and mythological relevance. By extension, Morrison's use of this technique has the effect of not only being a reflection of the psychological state of the individual, but also of the greater consciousness of contemporary Western Civilisation and its origins.

Another characteristic of his narrative style is that while Morrison's poetry clearly shows the influence of others (in a philosophical and stylistic sense), he manages to make it his own in the way he adapts these influences to his style, experiences, and ideas. We would expect to find remnants of quotes, stolen lines and ideas, in a lesser writer, but Morrison shows his strength as a poet by resisting plagiarism and blatant 'borrowing' in order to achieve originality in his own verse. As T. S. Eliot has said, 'Bad poets borrow, good poets steal.'

To the critic or the new reader of Morrison's poetry, perhaps the most difficult aspect of his verse is that it is very surreal at times, as well as highly symbolic. There is a pervading sense of the irrational, chaotic, and the violent; an effect produced by startling juxtapositions of images and words. Without a grasp of the central ideas and allusions behind his use of these tropes, the poems can seem like mere ramblings or fragments of word-play.

When I first encountered Morrison's poetry it became immediately apparent that it was not 'easy' to decipher the meaning behind the symbolism and metaphor. As I endeavoured to understand what it was that Morrison was actually conveying, I discovered that I could get a reasonably coherent grasp of the meaning by analysing three key things: (1) Contemporary (pop) culture references, (2) mythological (especially archetypal) allusion, and (3) philosophical reference and influence.

Once I realised that Morrison used a combination of these key tropes, the meaning behind the verse deepened and my reading was greatly enhanced because of this decoding. I have also used this strategy in my analysis of his poetry to reveal the carnivalesque world he created. A place peopled by characters and events straight out of Morrison's circus of the mind, drawn directly from the strange streets of Los Angeles and the conceptual realms of mythology, psychology and philosophy.

In the notes to Morrison's posthumous collection, *The American Night*,[2] we are told to 'trust the poet. Trust in the poet's genius and judgement, his craft and intelligence' (*AN*, pg. 205). In consideration of this suggestion I approached this study of Morrison's work and, after completion, this approach was justified in the revelation that he was indeed a competent and erudite poet. The 'notes' also provide a fairly accurate and succinct summation of Morrison's style, motifs and poetic, in relation to the challenges involved in deciphering the layered meaning in his poems:

> Frequently abstract, often layered with metaphors, similes and symbols, sometimes lacking apparent connection tissue, Jim's poetry confronted us with bold images and textures that were unwilling to reveal their

meaning to a casual reading. when a poem was obscure, we had to trust that the poet had purposefully made the shell hard to crack. to gain entry we would need to leave behind our preconceived notions of what a poem should be and open ourselves to what these poems were: bold, unconventional, experimental, difficult and startling.[3]

Morrison's speech is that of a native tongue, and his eye is that of a visionary American poet. He belongs to what poet and critic Jerome Rothenberg calls the 'American Prophecy . . . present in all that speaks to our sense of 'identity' and our need for renewal.' Rothenberg sees this prophetic tradition as:

"...affirming the oldest function of poetry, which is to interrupt the habits of ordinary consciousness by means of more precise and highly charged uses of language and to provide new tools for discovering the underlying relatedness of all life . . . A special concern for the interplay of myth and history runs through the whole of American literature. Thoreau, Emerson, and Whitman saw the poet's function in part as revealing the visionary meaning of our lives in relation to the time and place in which we live . . . we have taken this American emphasis on the relationship of myth and history, of poetry and life, as the central meaning of a 'prophetic' native tradition."[4]

This important aspect of his work and his commitment to his particular style (one closely aligned to Rothenberg's 'prophetic' tradition) is that it reveals his knowledge of the canon and his desire to be included among his contemporaries as being of that time in place in American literary and cultural history.

The lasting impression of Morrison's poems is that they attempt to render modern existence (in terms of words and imagery) as something akin to a chaotic nightmare that is inextricably linked to the foundation myths of Western Civilization. In this sense, he points to classic archetypes and folklore as both an antidote and a reason for modern society's ills. He has something important to say and he chooses to convey his thoughts in a way that requires an effort of understanding and commitment. He could have chosen to write what he wanted with simple prose, instead he chose the medium of free-verse poetry to emphasise the necessity of myth and the complexity and difficulty of modern existence.

I. Critiquing the Myth of Morrison

'He who fights with monsters should be careful lest he thereby become a monster. And if thou gaze long into an abyss, the abyss will also gaze into thee.' (§ 146)

Friedrich Nietzsche, *Beyond Good and Evil*

In 1994, Professor of French Literature at Duke University, Wallace Fowlie, published the first 'scholarly' study of the poetry of the charismatic lead singer of the sixties rock band The Doors. *Rimbaud & Jim Morrison: The Rebel as Poet*,[1] as suggested by the title, is a comparative study of the lives and work of Arthur Rimbaud and Jim Morrison. The fact that Morrison had written to Fowlie, thanking him for his 1966 translation, *Rimbaud: Complete Works, Selected Letters*,[2] proved the starting point for Fowlie's comparison between the two poets.

Despite Fowlie's apparently good intentions, his knowledge of Rimbaud's work and his understanding of French symbolism far outweigh any of the observations he makes about Morrison's poetry. Fowlie elects to use recourse to classical myth when he makes observations about Morrison, much like the majority of newspaper and magazine articles that mined the prevalent archetypal image of the drunken poet/performer as a Grecian bacchanalian god.

However, instead of using the media's prevailing alignment of Jim with Dionysus,[3] Fowlie instead prefers to emphasise a different aspect of his (Morrison's) character as a point of difference (I assume). For example, he labels Morrison 'Kouros,' the Greek word for 'a youth attractive to men and women. At times in praise of his beauty. At other times it [the word] is hurled almost as a curse at those youths who insolently torment older people.(*Rimbaud*, p.105)[4]

After inadvertently making his own contribution to the Morrison 'myth' by stereotyping him as Kouros, Fowlie goes on to disclaim his own observation by stating that '[t]his name I suggest as representative of the non-hypocritical innocence of Jim when he was not aware of the power of his appearance and his personality.' (p. 105) When was Morrison ever *not* aware of his appearance and his personality? Preteens?

This is a typical example of Fowlie's misunderstanding of Morrison's character and is, unfortunately, what informs most of his discussion of Morrison's poetry. Consequently, Fowlie only ever illumines the obvious in the poems, although he does make solid connections between some of Morrison's poems and their allusion to and the influence of Rimbaud. Perhaps the most valuable aspect of Fowlie's study, as indicated by the back-cover description, is that it provides:

> . . . a glimpse of the affinities and resemblances between European literary traditions and American rock music and youth culture in the late twentieth century.

Fowlie *has* written a perceptive analysis of Rimbaud's poetry and the poet's role as rebel, similar to the observations he presented in his 1946 study: *Rimbaud: The Myth of Childhood.*[5] Unfortunately, however, *Rimbaud & Jim Morrison* fails as an exegesis on Morrison's poetry because of Fowlie's preoccupation with aligning the two poets in terms of their character via select samples of their work and biographies. By concentrating on the myth of Morrison, as he previously did with Rimbaud, Fowlie ignores the literary qualities of the poetry and elects to construct a character study instead.

Like most people who encountered Morrison, either through books or in person, Fowlie never seems to get past the myth. In view of this unfortunate aspect of his discussion, his approach towards Morrison's poetry is superficial and is more memoir than serious critique.

Despite the fact that this first 'serious' study is more comparative biography than literary analysis, what Fowlie *does* provide is a superficial guide to those wanting to pursue certain points, such as the influence of Nietzsche, Artaud, Rimbaud and the 'Beat' writers on Morrison's own writing.

Most literature on Morrison is predominantly biographical, preferring to regurgitate the myth and scandal surrounding his life and times, rather than give his art any serious consideration. In light of the fact that Morrison's wish, toward the end of his life, was to be regarded as a serious poet separated from the myth of the Dionysian pop star, my own study choses to use the prevalence of mythic allusion in his work to inform the meaning of the text, rather than to ascribe a character trait of the poet. It is within this context (i.e. Morrison's literary aspirations) that this study endeavours to provide a good starting point for further serious study and, hopefully, an enlightening analysis of his literary work.

Despite interest, both negative and positive, his writing has not been comprehensively analysed in the context of his life and the broader American culture. Nor has it been discussed in terms of its merits (and failings), or its place in the ranks of American literature. The reasons why are twofold.

Firstly, Morrison's verse is obscure, highly subjective and at times obscene or grotesque in imagery and speech, as in 'An American Prayer' from *The American Night:* [6]

> *Cling to cunts & cocks*
> *of despair*
> *We got our final vision*
> *by clap*
> *Columbus' groin got*

filled w/ green death

*(I touched her thigh
& death smiled)*

(*AN*, p.5)

Secondly, the 'myth' tends to impede any progress past itself — the romantic idea of Morrison as 'poet-performer' is preferable to the critics than any serious attempt to actually understand or analyse the poetry itself. For example, Fowlie's judgement of Morrison's life pigeonholes him in terms of the poetry; he cannot separate Morrison's poetry from the 'persona [which] had everything to do with the principle of Dionysus.'[7]

To this point, Morrison's reputation typically precedes any serious literary analysis of the work. Despite his failings as a human and as a poet, it is my contention that he left behind some valuable and important examples of his poetic talent that deserve serious analysis.

It is my belief that Morrison's best poetry shows a strength and significance which situates him as an important poet in the American literary tradition. The discussion ahead focusses primarily on Morrison's earliest work to reveal the ideas, influences, and allusions that he skilfully synthesised into his own poetic voice. Hopefully, what I have found will provide a frame of reference for further study. The search for meaning in Morrison's work, being the primary focus that underpins this introduction to his poetry.

II. Motivation & Motif

'I decided that it was not wisdom that enabled [poets] to write their poetry, but a kind of instinct or inspiration, such as you find in seers and prophets who deliver all their sublime messages without knowing in the least what they mean.'

Socrates

Morrison's early experiments with poetry and prose reveal some intellectually ambitious ideas about aesthetics, philosophy, life, and film (in particular). Written over a five-year period (1964-69), the poems also show a strong influence in concept and style, ranging from the philosophies of Nietzsche and Blake to the avant-garde writings of the Surrealists and the 'Beat' authors. Whatever influences and concerns may have shaped his aesthetic and philosophical values, his early writings are the foundation on which he developed his poetical style. All the motifs, symbols, and imagery introduced in his first collection of poems recur continuously throughout his later works.

Originally conceived as two separate books, *The Lords and The New Creatures* [1] was published as a single volume, containing a mixture of Morrison's philosophies and poetry. Essentially, it is a forum for the fleshing out of ideas and style. The first half of the book *The Lords: Notes on Vision*, is a collection of notes and prose poems while the second half, *The New Creatures*, is an assortment of poetry.

The Lords is a motley work of ideas and prose, loosely held together with motifs of death, cinema, and the reinterpretation of mythical and theatrical theory. While originality seems to be in short supply and naïve idealism in abundance, the content is interesting because of the allusion, selection, and presentation of ideas and philosophy that are most influential to Morrison.

Stylistically, *The Lords* reflects his propensity for 'dark' imagery and self-mythology, which would later be a fundamental characteristic of his poetry and stage performances. Pervading motifs used regularly throughout his poetry, as much as they are used as poetic devices, also reflect his personal preoccupations and connections with his own philosophy: the 'city,' 'love,' 'sex,'[2] 'death,' 'assassins,' 'voyeurs,' 'wanderers,' 'deserts,' 'shamanism,' and so on.

The autobiographical and historical references in the poems reflect the myth-making process of turning fact into fiction. As events that shaped his life and consciousness are translated into material for the poems, the poetry becomes a mythological rendering of Morrison's interior psychological world.

His itinerant childhood constantly spent shifting around the country, combined with his career choice of international rock star, prompt Morrison to identify himself with the image of the vagabond or wanderer. He uses this literary figure/device in his poetry as it obviously has symbolic and poetic appeal, as well as personal significance. As he has suggested of himself and others: 'We're like actors, turned loose in this world to wander in search of a phantom, endlessly searching for a half-formed shadow of our lost reality.'[3]

His poetry, however, has a strong sense of place; the strong observational power of the astute outsider, works well in the invocations of strange border towns and locations. His vision of Los Angeles, or 'L'america' is profound in its focus and impressions. It is even stranger because of the ambivalent nostalgia Morrison seems to hold for the place, where he had lived and performed with the Doors: 'Los Angeles is a city looking for a ritual to join its fragments.'[4]

At first, for Morrison, it was musical theatre that would attempt to provide the 'ritual' for the city, using his shaman principles to try to 'join its fragments', and bring his audience together. When that failed, and the 'summer of love' and the notion of hippie solidarity had dissipated, he turned to his poetry as the ritual that would piece together the fragments of his *own* experience. Like Eliot's 'fragments' shored against his ruins in *The Waste Land*, Morrison's words and poetry are the means by which he can make sense of his world and guard against his aesthetic mortality.

However, as always in his poems, there is a sense of cynicism, directed toward himself as well as the reader. Almost as if, his suffering and sacrifices, made in the name of art and cultural freedom, were not for his own benefit but for the benefit of 'you,' the reader:

Words are healing.

Words got me the wound
& will get me well [⁵]

If you believe it.

(AN, p. 61)

This segment from his absurdly titled poem, 'Lament for the Death of my Cock,' reflects Morrison's pessimism and poetic idealism. The sense of suffering expressed in this later poem is also found in his earlier work *The Lords*, in relation to the idea of sacrifice for the good of all: 'What sacrifice, at what price can the city be born?'

Morrison's early awareness of society's ills, and his benevolent sense of social responsibility, meant that he had a personally doomed and intense experience of America and its ideals. In particular, the 'Western Dream,' as expressed in his apocalyptic invocation of a 'brave new world' of dreamlike existence and ritual: 'We are from the West. The world we suggest should be a new Wild West, a sensuous, evil world, strange, and haunting.'[6]

With his own experience informing his work, Morrison begins *The Lords* by addressing the reader rhetorically, as if revealing some truth about modern existence. He introduces his analogy of a society's relation to place, in terms of a 'game' that takes place within the city.

Morrison's motif of the city is as surrealistic as it is symbolist in the strange juxtapositions of vivid imagery, symbol, and metaphors of human consciousness. It is as modernist in its urban reaction to the self and its distillation of many locales, as it is post-modern in its dissolution of the barriers between the individual and their surroundings.

Throughout Morrison's poetry, the city is a place of despair, a place to escape from, an ominous source of disease and death. Nevertheless, it is his primary source for a motley assortment of bizarre characters and experiences from the 'dark' side. This conceptualisation of the city as a dystopian environment seems to represent the American condition and, by extension, all Western civilisations. The city, for Morrison, is a metaphorical reflection of society:

We all live in the city.

The city forms — often physically, but inevitably psychically— a circle. A Game. A ring of death with sex at its center. Drive toward outskirts of city suburbs. At the edge discover zones of sophisticated vice and boredom, child prostitution. But in the grimy ring immediately surrounding the daylight business district exists the only real crowd life of our mound, the only street life, night life. Diseased specimens in dollar hotels, low boarding houses, bars, pawn shops, burlesques and brothels, in dying arcades which never die, in streets and streets of all-night cinemas.

(*L*, pg. 3)

Like Eliot's invocation of the 'unreal city' in *The Waste Land*, inherited from Baudelaire's line about the '[s]warming city, city full of dreams, where ghost's in broad daylight catch the walker's sleeve',[7] there is a relation of person to place. Rimbaud's perception of a city is more in line with Morrison's, when he cries: 'O sorrowful city! O city now struck dumb, / Head and heart stretched out in paleness / In endless doorways thrown wide by time; / City the Dismal Past can only bless: / Body galvanised for sufferings yet to come.'[8] The modern city, for Morrison, is also a deathly and haunted place:

> *Cancer city*
> *Urban fall*
> *Summer sadness*
> *The highways of the town*
> *Ghosts in cars*
> *Electric shadows*

(*NC*, 18)

The city is diseased – crumbling. Its citizens patrol the highways like zombies, 'ghosts.' He seems to suggest that those who enter the city become part of the cancer or somehow die from its effects. Cancer and leprosy, much like his concept of the city, seem to have synonymous meaning for Morrison as a metaphor for the larger society/American/Western civilisation.

The city is a 'connector' for Morrison, a universal place where humanity is represented in all its failings and dreams. Of course, the city is also an extended metaphor or conceit that is never far from a natural counterpart, in this case a bee-hive, spider-web, and sliced ant-hill. The population are all descendants of the same species. The use of this conceit enables Morrison to push the reader to a more sophisticated understanding of his concept of the city and, ultimately, his notions of 'The Lords' and 'The New Creatures':

> The City. *Hive. Web, or severed insect mound. All citizens heirs of the same royal parent.*
>
> (*NC*, 18)

Morrison's motif of the city is as surrealistic as it is symbolic in the strange juxtapositions of vivid imagery, symbol, and metaphors of human consciousness. Throughout Morrison's poetry, the city appears paradoxically as a place of despair, yet a place where experiences of sensuality and euphoric indulgence abound. It is a place of malaise and tensions, yet it offers art and life as well as an ominous source of disease and death.

Nevertheless, this place of binaries and complexity is his primary source for an assortment of bizarre characters and experiences from the 'dark' side. It is a place where the 'Lords' and the 'New [suggesting modern] Creatures' cohabit. In this regard, the 'Lords' represent the old guard which is the oppressive culture of authoritarian rule and close-minded conformity. Whereas, the 'New Creatures' are the generation who seek enlightenment and freedom by way of personal transformation.

Morrison's notion of American society and its effect upon culture and people is one of the main concepts behind *The Lords*. He emphasises the negative and dehumanising aspects of modern society as being, essentially, an existential quagmire that has contributed to a lack of any real spiritual or meaningful dimension. The 'Lords,' however, are those who have been able to seperate themselves from the masses, be it by positions of power and hierarchy, and who are in control of the culture by way of media, politics, and authoritarian power.

These 'Lords' control those who are content to be followers and are willing to suffer silently. In one of the last interviews he gave before his death, Morrison reflects upon his earlier conception of the lords in his earlier poetry:

> …the feeling of powerlessness and helplessness that people have in the face of reality. They have no real control over events or their own lives. Something is controlling them. The closest they ever get is the television set. In creating this idea of the lords, it also came to reverse itself. Now to me, the lords mean something entirely different. I couldn't really explain. It's like the opposite. Somehow the lords are a romantic race of people who have found a

way to control their environment and their own lives. They're somehow different from other people.[9]

The notion of the 'Lords' is a philosophical construct and a poetical device used to distinguish society as hierarchical. Morrison's idea of the lords can be related to Nietzsche's view in *The Will to Power* (1967), of 'the Lords of the Earth — that higher species which would climb aloft to new and impossible things, to a broader vision, and to its task on earth.' Whereas Nietzsche's lords are the poets and artists — the people who are revolutionaries, who seek to change the conformist culture in which they exist and lead society forward (akin to Morrison's conception of the shaman which is discussed in detail later in this study), Morrison's Lords are the oppressors. They are the antithesis of Nietzsche's concept in that their unified goal is to suppress innovation and individual freedom, rather than promoting it:

> *The Lords*. Events take place beyond our knowledge or control. Our lives are lived for us. We can only try to enslave others. But gradually, special perceptions are being developed. The idea of the 'Lords' is beginning to form in some minds. We should enlist them into bands of perceivers to tour the labyrinth during their mysterious nocturnal appearances. The Lords have secret entrances, and they know disguises. But they give themselves away in minor ways. Too much glint of light in the eye. A wrong gesture. Too long and curious a glance.

(L, p. 32)

This flipping, if you will, of Nietzsche's concept on its head, suggests either a misreading on Morrison's part or, more likely, an amalgamation of his own, more contemporary viewpoint, as an extension of the idea.[10] What ties Morrison's conception of the Lords together, and what ultimately makes his own concept a credo for his artistic pursuits, is that he identifies the practice of art (specifically imagist) as being the key, both as central tenets to the Lords *and* the New creatures.

The Lords use art to control, manipulate and subjugate the masses and the New Creatures use art (music, painting, poetry, etc.), as an experiential tool which, ultimately, leads to freedom by way of enlightenment or self-awareness:

> The Lords appease us with images. They give us books, concerts, galleries, shows, cinemas. Especially the cinemas. Through art they confuse us and blind us to our enslavement. Art adorns our prison walls, keeps us silent and diverted and indifferent.

(L, p. 32)

Morrison's concept of the New Creatures, is not as clear as his conception of the Lords. Once again, nothing is black and white with Morrison and the astute reader will discover that *The Lords and New Creatures* has two very distinct parts. The first section of *The Lords* is a collection of prose in the form of vignettes, epigraphs, and aphorisms — some of which read like prose poems, while most seem to be written as notes. The second section is composed mainly of free-verse poetry that has clear structure and composition.

Why the difference in style? Why the explanation of his concept of 'the Lords' and then no clear definition of the 'New Creatures'? The clue is in the presentation of the work.

As explained above, the Lords are depicted in the first section as an amalgam of ideas and allusion representing those who control society; relayed in prose-form, these notions are communicated as notes or reportage and are fairly clear in their descriptions as literal interpretations.

The concept of the New Creatures, however, is much more figurative and metaphorical and definitely not as clear-cut. The New Creature, in this regard is represented by the poet himself and the poetry. The first stanza indicates the presence of the New Creature:

> *Snakeskin Jacket*
> *Indian eyes*
> *Brilliant hair*
>
> *He moves in disturbed*
> *Nile Insect*
> *Air*

(*NC*, I, pg. 3)

The direct allusion to himself is obvious; the 'Lizard King' *is* the New Creature and the poetry is the vehicle he has used to transport himself back and forward through time. His is not a contemporary realm per se, due largely to the highly symbolic and visionary quality of the verse. This mystical aspect of the poetry is peppered with reference and allusion to the oldest myths and civilisations: Aztec, Egypt, the Orient, Africa, and America are all referenced and placed within a post-Edenic world that is in a state of violent and chaotic upheaval.

Morrison seamlessly blends the archaic with the contemporary, as his characters journey through biblical swamps and deserts seeking escape from the oppressive Lords and, ultimately, emancipation. In this regard, Morrison suggests that the poet-seer's life and art are and should be informed by the oldest myths and legends.

The world of *the New Creatures* is a mystical and chaotic one, filled with violence, oppression endanger at every turn and it is the poet who will relay the experience through visionary poetry that will signal the new direction. This is Morrison's *Wasteland* and it is bleak and disturbing.

The overall impression of the second section is that the poems warn that the road to enlightenment and freedom, is fraught with suffering and hardship:

> *deceit smiles*
> *incredible hardships are suffered*

by those barely able
to endure

(*NC*, pg. 30 - 1/89)

    The concerns and motifs in *The Lords and New Creatures* will inform Morrison's later work and it is there (in *Wilderness* and *The American Night*) that we will find the explication and resolution of some of these core themes. In the proceeding chapters, the transition between Morrison's less adept fleshing out of thought and poetical style, to a more mature philosophical and aesthetic stance, will become apparent.

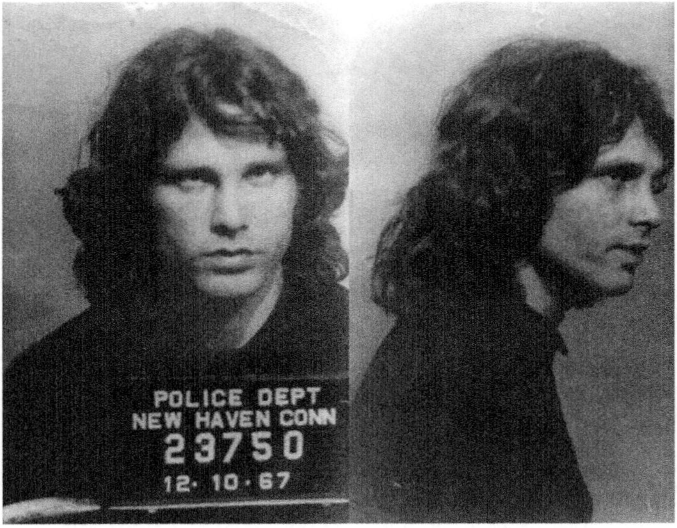
POLICE DEPT
NEW HAVEN CONN
23750
12· 10 · 67

III. Philosophy, Poetry, & America

'Follow your bliss and the universe will open doors for you where there were only walls.'

Joseph Campbell

To decode Morrison's poetry, we need to recognise the philosophy that informs and underlies the meaning, symbolism, imagery, and theme. The philosophy is primarily Nietzschean in origin, although the poetry is not singular in its allegiance to the European philosopher. Rather, Morrison adapts variations of Nietzsche's philosophy to correlate with his own experience as expressed within the verse.

In other words, the philosophical system behind the meaning of the poem is not really a system as such, but more of a set of ideas which Morrison draws upon for inspiration.

Morrison's various biographers concur that he read and revered the works of Friedrich Nietzsche. In the most widely read biography of Morrison's life, *No*

One here Gets Out Alive, the authors attest to the fact that Morrison 'devoured Friedrich Nietzsche, the poetic German philosopher whose views on aesthetics, morality, and the Apollonian-Dionysian duality would appear again and again in Jim's conversation, poetry, songs, and life.'[1]

John Densmore, the percussionist in The Doors, wrote in his memoir *Riders on the Storm* that 'Nietzsche killed Jim Morrison . . . Morrison the Superman, the Dionysian madman, the Birth of Tragedy himself.'[2]

Ray Manzarek, the organist of The Doors, also remembers 'walks in the soft shore break of Venice Beach discussing Nietzsche's Birth of Tragedy' with Morrison.[3]

Morrison himself, revealingly suggested to New York Magazine reporter Richard Goldstein in an interview, that he should 'read Nietzsche on the nature of tragedy to understand where he's really at.' [Goldstein noted that] His eyes glow as he launches into a discussion of the Apollonian-Dionysian struggle for control of the life force.'[4]

Pervading Morrison's work is an unshakeable dedication to Nietzsche's ideas on aesthetics and human nature. Intermingled with this influence is a loyalty to the theatrical manifestos of Antonin Artaud and The Living Theatre Company, and an understanding and empathy with the poetic dictums of visionary poets such as Rimbaud and William Blake. These influences form an underlying blend of philosophy that informs Morrison's own words and actions. He welds philosophy, myth, and his own contemporary perspective of culture, society, and the world into his poetical 'vision'.

Using an everyday symbol of modern existence, such as television or the cinema, he associates it with the timeless philosophical and existential subject of life: 'the attraction of the cinema lies in the fear of death.'[5]

Combined with the excesses of an age where stimulants, sex, quasi-religion, and cultural revolution are the norm, it is both surprising and understandable that he had such a consistently borderline nihilistic tone in his verse:

> *We live, we die*
> *& death not ends it*
> *Journey we more into the*
> *Nightmare . . .*

> *We're reaching for death*
> *on the end of a candle*
> *We're trying for something*
> *that's already found us . . .*

> *Do you know how pale & wanton thrillful*
> *comes death on a strange hour*
> *unannounced, unplanned for*
> *like a scaring over-friendly guest you've*
> *brought to bed*
> *Death makes angels of us all*
> *& gives us wings*
> *where we had shoulders*
> *smooth as raven's*
> *claws*

(*AN*, pp. 4-10)

Simultaneously (and paradoxically), a relentless optimism pervades. In 'An American Prayer,' the poet calls for life to be invigorated and made sensual by the turning away from a chaotic present, sick with the throes of materialism and war, to a mythic past full of meaning and example:

> *Let's reinvent the gods, all the myths*
> *of the ages*
> *Celebrate symbols from deep elder forests*
> *{Have you forgotten the lessons*
> *of the ancient war}*
>
> *We need great golden copulations*

(*AN*, pp. 3-18)

Despite the fact that in 'Notebook Poems'[6] and 'Paris Journal'[7] his poetry is concise and profound in the clarity of expression, imagery, and tone; depression clouds Morrison's later work. The verse is simple, emotional, and pessimistic—an honest depiction of a melancholic and resigned reality. A poem such as 'If Only I' expresses Morrison's existentialism in a confessional mode very similar to other poets of his day. The narrator of the poem laments the loss of his self, and then the illusion of the notion of 'self.' The poet's disillusionment with life, has reached the point where he can not even 'feel' himself to determine the validity of his own existence:

> *If only I*
> *could feel*
> *The sound*
> *of the sparrows*
> *& feel childhood*
> *pulling me*
> *back again*
>
> *If only I could feel*
> *me pulling back*
> *again*
> *& feel embraced*
> *by reality*
> *again*
> *I would die*
> *Gladly die*

(*AN*, p. 187)

Morrison's self-conscious portrayal of the suffering of an anguished poet, paused on the edge of the abyss of the self, is a symbolic expression of an ultimately destructive conflict between birth and death. It is a resolutely sad search for an ideal, for 'one last chance at bliss' — a record of the distance between an ordinary human and Nietzsche's *ubermensch*. Invariably, Morrison's words reflect Nietzsche's own sentiments and poetry found in 'Entflohn die Holden Traume' ('Fled Are the Lovely Dreams'):

Fled are the lovely dreams
Fled is the past . . .

I have never experienced
The joy and happiness of life.
I look back sadly
Upon times that are long vanished . . .

I do not know what I believe
Or why I am still living. For what?
I would like to die, die — . . .[8]

The fact that Morrison's death looks increasingly like a heroin overdose, gives the above mentioned poem and his earlier poems an autobiographical significance in relation to the ideals and philosophies that governed his life.

Whatever the cause of Morrison's death, it could be argued that his demise was the logical result of a combination of self-destructive excess and aesthetic idealism. The existential abyss that yawned in front of him finally swallowed him up after years of heavy drinking, drug-taking, touring and a seemingly unshakeable adherence to the Blakean/Rimbaudian mantra that: 'the road of excess leads to the palace of wisdom.'

Ironically, and somewhat prophetically, in *The Lords*, he frequently speaks of death, fate, and the consequences of the 'game':

> *When play dies it becomes the Game.*
> *When sex dies it becomes Climax.*
> *All games contain the idea of death . . .*
>
> (L, pp. 3-4)

> *French Deck.* Solitary stroker of cards. He dealt himself a hand. Turn stills of the past in unending permutations, shuffle and begin. Sort the images again. And sort them again. This game reveals germs of truth, and death.
>
> (L, p. 16)

This understanding of death reflects an existential world-view (as in his poem 'If Only I') and a belief in the ultimate sacrifice/demise of the 'outsider' artist with who Morrison identified himself. Sex is the connector to the physical, to the realm of the real, populated by other 'players' in the game. Love or attachment to another, is an emotional experience which leads to a metaphorical death of the self, in the very act of coitus or ejaculation. Denial of the self is the consequence of not experiencing the 'void' (or the 'abyss') of the self. As Morrison himself suggests: 'Love is one of the handful of devices we have to avoid the void, so to speak.'[9]

Morrison's sense of isolation is complete in his concept of the game — it has become an existential conceit in its presentation of an inescapable net of death, where the truest performance of the individual (artist) is not only necessary but somehow futile in the larger scheme of things. The paradoxical nature of the 'game' of art (and by extension, life), is made more explicit when Morrison states that: 'a game is a closed field, a ring of death with sex at the centre, and performing is the only game I've got.'[10]

Whatever the implications, it is ultimately an acknowledgement of the solipsistic nature of the poet/artist, the sacrifices that must be made in the pursuit of art, and the psychological pain of giving birth to a new self.

Morrison, develops his romantic concept of the artistic outsider by suggesting that the true aesthete must transform reality with art and, by extension, the art must then transform the audience. In order to construct a consciousness that is capable of true self-realisation and peak artistic practice, the confrontation of harsh reality must occur within the psychological inner-dimensions of the artist.

Ironically, this ascetic ideal can only be attained by withdrawal from the 'real' world and in turn the giving up of sensual pleasures, of which Morrison was so fond. He is seeming aware of this tautologous relationship between personal artistic and spiritual growth, and sacrifice:

> Urge to come to terms with the 'Outside,' by absorbing, interiorizing it. I won't come out, you must come in to me. Into my womb-garden where I peer out. Where I can construct a universe within the skull, to rival the real.

(*L*, p.14)

He concludes this section in *Lords* with the epigraph: 'You cannot touch these phantoms' (*L*, p.15), as if he were acknowledging the difficulty in attaining any ascetic level as long as one is driven by desires, as if the aphorisms and ideas contained therein are unique to his character.

Similar to the metaphorical imagery in Nietzsche's *Thus Spoke Zarathustra*, Morrison uses the womb as a symbol of the earth, the place where, like a flower or a 'clay man,' the superman or 'ubermensch' is born. It is a goal and a belief that we are capable as humans of constructing a heightened existence by the destruction of the old self or reality.

It is an ideal, very much a part of the Morrison myth, and the American myth that through self-destruction comes enlightenment, transcendence of the 'unnatural' societal-self. This 'creative destruction' is also evident in the lives of other American literary figures like Kerouac, William Burroughs, and Hart Crane.

Another interesting connection to Nietzsche is Morrison's use of the metaphor of the Edenic garden/gardener, as a kind of internalised organic place/state of being, or symbolic representation of the intellectual or creative genius. In *Daybreak*, Nietzsche draws a similar parallel to Morrison's 'womb-garden' — between 'thinker' and the earthy allegorical figure of the 'Gardener' and garden:

> Out of damp and gloomy days, out of solitude, out of loveless words directed at us, *conclusions* grow up in us like fungus: one morning they are there, we know not how, and they gaze upon us, morose and grey. Woe to the thinker who is not the gardener but only the soil of the plants that grow in him![11]

For Morrison, the transformation of subjective experience into art lies at the core of his aesthetic philosophy and a driving force behind his preference to be a poet, rather than a pop-idol/performer. Perhaps he felt that what he could say on paper, was more of a truer artistic expression than what he could sing on stage.

Themes of power and violence in *The Lords and The New Creatures* were also part of the dark aspect of the '60s. Morrison's song lyrics that spoke as much about death as they did about love were associated with an end of an era. With the Vietnam War in full flight, Civil Rights protests, and assassinations, the death of hippie naiveté was imminent. Morrison himself sums up the reasons why things had changed:

> It's different now. (Pause) It used to seem possible to generate a movement — people rising up and joining together in a mass protest — refusing to be repressed any longer — like, they'd all put their strength together to break what Blake calls 'the mind forged manacles' . . . [t]he love-street times are dead. Sure, it's possible for there to be a

transcendence — but not on a mass level, not a universal rebellion. Now it has to take place on an individual level — every man for himself, as they say save yourself. Violence isn't always evil. What's evil is the infatuation with violence. [12]

The end of the '60s was characterised by an exalting of passion over intellect, body over mind, the perverse over the normal, the risks of violence and disaster over normal modes of existence. When asked by an interviewer his opinion on the social climate of America in the late '60s, Morrison summed up the feelings of a generation and the effects of cultural change on the nation:

I think for many people, especially city dwellers, it's a state of constant paranoia. Paranoia is defined as an irrational fear, but what if the paranoia is real? Then you just cope with it second by second.[13]

As a poet of his time, and as someone with a sensitive social consciousness, Morrison makes his poems reflect the age and place in which he writes. Yet, he does so in a way that makes a current event seem timeless, even ancient in its cloak of metaphorical language.

In *The Lords*, what is possibly a simple interpretation of the savage Tate-LaBianca killings by Charles Manson and his followers is turned into an archetypal image of the power of violence. Their capture in Death Valley California, hiding out in caves after the murders, waiting for their apocalyptic race war ('Helter Skelter') to begin, is reflected in

Morrison's perception of the media events of his day:

> *It takes large murder to turn rocks in the shade*
> *and expose strange worms beneath. The*
> > *lives of*
> *our discontented madmen are revealed.*

(*L*, p. 4)

Within the context of the surrounding poems, we recognise other significant events in American cultural and political history. In 'Baths, bars, the indoor pool. / Our injured leader lies prone on the tile,' we can find a reference to the death of Brian Jones[14] who drowned in a swimming pool.

Kennedy's assassination is mentioned: 'Modern circles of hell: Oswald (?) kills President,' and indirectly the Vietnam war and 'people burdened by historical events or dying in a bad landscape.' The more these references are turned over, like 'rocks in the shade,' the greater the depth and significance of meaning revealed in the verse.

The mere fact that these events are transcribed and incorporated into his poems signal that they were of a significance to Morrison in one way or another. The incorporation of personal and historical events is a core motif in Morrison's early poetry, and one that he would continue to use in his later works. It is also because of this cultural transcription, that Morrison's poetry has inherent value, in that it can be read as the record of an observer and very much a part of the era in which it was produced.

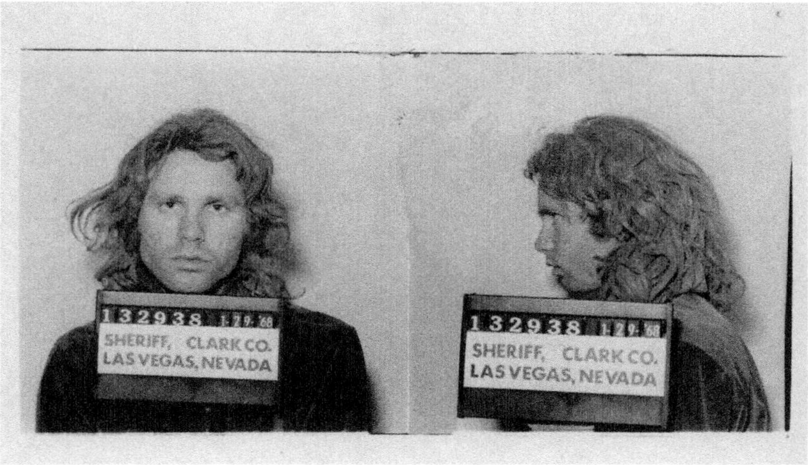

132938 1-29-68
SHERIFF, CLARK CO.
LAS VEGAS, NEVADA
132938 1-29-68
SHERIFF, CLARK CO.
LAS VEGAS, NEVADA

IV. Poetic & Poet

'Only those who will risk going too far can possibly find out how far one can go.'

T.S. Eliot

In contrast to *The Lords*, Morrison's companion text *The New Creatures*, emphasises the nightmarish existence of other 'creatures' who are submissive and almost sub-species in their herd mentality and hellish existence. The violent imagery and surreal nature of the verse in *The New Creatures*, creates a disorganised and chaotic collection of poetry that seems to have no apparent motive or logic.

The content is highly subjective and foreign to most readers; some allusions and imagery are familiar in their generality, yet pointless in the apparent obscurity and juxtaposition. The poems' personal content unfortunately makes most of *The New Creatures* inaccessible in their metaphorical and symbolic rendition of Morrison's psyche. In parts, Morrison evokes a tone and a cadence with the structure of word and image interplay similar in effectiveness to the lyrics he wrote for The Doors, some of which he actually performed:

> *Ensenada*
> *the dead seal*
> *the dog crucifix*
> *Ghosts of the dead car sun.*
> *Stop the car.*
> *Rain. Night.*
> *Feel.*
>
> (NC, p. 18)

Most of the poems in *The New Creatures* seem strange and unrelated. Morrison gives the reader a clue to his method of poetry, by his comments on art forms like film, especially when his poetry is so obviously cinematic in its style and effect. He states, with a reference to the modernist idea of art replicating 'stream of consciousness,' that he was 'interested in film because, to me, it's the closest approximation in art that we have to the actual flow of consciousness.'[1]

Many of Morrison's poems throughout his work *are* like film-clips in an avant-garde surrealist cinema. There is an intellectual, yet dreamy quality to his juxtaposition of ideas and insights about the world.

Like the main technique of crowd manipulation he used on stage, Morrison uses the pause for great effect, yet not in the conventional grammatical or formal sense. Instead of a caesura, an ellipse, or a new line (all of which he also uses to effect), he uses an image as a barrier to overcome, to be 'broken through':

> *Savage destiny*
>
> *Naked girl, seen from behind,*
> *on a natural road*
>
> *Friends*
> *explore the labyrinth*
>
> *— Movie*
> *young woman left on the desert*
>
> *A city gone mad w/ fever*
>
> (*NC*, p. 12)

This pause, this break in flow or subject (in this case the metaphorical 'labyrinth') renders the verse as a staccato series of images, rather than a progressive stream of ideas and words. In other words, the structure of the poem does try to replicate the irrational logic of stream of consciousness.

Often, these poems differentiate themselves from Morrison's more coherent verse by their abstract nature; characteristically, they are like surreal paintings of violent and bizarre scenes, giving the reader a sense of the intoxicated state prevalent throughout much of Morrison's notorious, alcoholic and drug-abused, life.

While, in underlining this connection between Morrison's poetry and cultural and personal events, I risk implying that his work is simply autobiographical rather than aspiring to a 'higher' artistic realm, it is important to consider that some of the best works of literature use the same technique to emphasis the truth and relevance behind the vision presented. T.S. Eliot's *Four Quartets* comes to mind.

Reading some of Morrison's less adept poetry, is like reading notes someone took while experiencing an LSD trip. The failings of some of his earlier poetry are evident in the over-use of this highly obscure and symbolic imagery, which has the unfortunate effect of distancing most readers from his work. While this aspect of the early poems makes it difficult to not only decipher any implied meaning, it also interrupts the flow of the poetry due to the effect on the reader. The resulting confusion suggests that some of these early poems were either 'over-worked' or were, perhaps, not considered for a wider audience.

However, what these poems do provide is an interesting record of the young poet's fleshing out of ideas and motifs as he developed and matured as a poet.

The same elements (which make some of the earlier poems difficult to read), combine in his more proficient poetry to produce a more interesting effect: in intonation, profound visions, states of consciousness, and hallucinatory images, all culminating in a unique contemplation of the world. His cinematic technique of image juxtaposition also emulates the effects of a 'psychedelic' experience, which could also be interpreted as no less than an experience of Morrison's world and the '60s itself.

Morrison's idealised and romantic notion of the role of the poet (and poetry) was the genesis for most of his experience. Poetry inspired and vocalised his love of the cinematic, performance art, and musical lyricism (via the songs he wrote and performed with The Doors). It also expressed his most profound thoughts, philosophies, and beliefs.

Poetry was a means to relay his world in a symbolic language steeped in traditional and mythological recourse. The obvious appeal of such a medium, for Morrison, was that he viewed poetry as one of the most enduring forms of art and a means of affecting change. Moreover, he also saw poetry as a means of continuing tradition, history, and art. As he himself said of poetry:

> . . . real poetry doesn't say anything, it just ticks off the possibilities. Opens all doors. You can walk through any one that suits you . . . and that's why poetry appeals to me so much — because it's so eternal. As long as there are people, they can remember words and combinations of words. Nothing else can survive a holocaust but poetry and songs. No one can remember an entire novel . . . but so long as there are human beings, songs and poetry can continue. If my poetry aims to achieve anything, it's to deliver people from the limited ways in which they see and feel.[2]

In *The American Night*, his poem 'An American Prayer'[3] echoes Sir James Frazer's *Golden Bough* along with the philosophies of Artaud and Nietzsche. Morrison appeals in his lament for understanding, for a consensus that technology and so-called 'progress' is not necessarily better or more exciting than the mythically imbued past:

> *Let's reinvent the gods, all the myths*
> *of the ages*
> *Celebrate symbols from deep elder forests . . .*
>
> *We have assembled inside this ancient*
> *& insane theatre*
> *To propagate our lust for life*
> *& flee the swarming wisdom*
> *of the streets . . .*
> *I'm sick of dour faces*
> *Staring at me from the T.V.*
> *Tower. I want roses in*
> *My garden bower; dig?*

(*AN*, pp. 3-18)

In this sense, his attitude toward modernity is one of disdain, similar to Eliot's perception of a defunct Western civilisation in *The Waste Land*. Consistently, throughout his poems, Morrison is anti-TV, almost as if he sees it as responsible for contemporary society's decline. It is paradoxical in that he vehemently supports a view of the world through the camera lens of the filmmaker's eye.

Apart from this cinematic motif that carries

through from his earliest work, the consistent use of dark and violent symbols and imagery, and the allusion to myth, philosophy and art, there is no one clear unifying aspect to his poetry. While there may be discernible, and repetitive, symbolism, mythological allusion, and the use of certain literary devices, one singular commonality remains to be found.

There is, however, an element of autobiography in most of the poems, subtly evoked in the symbols and motifs associated with the lead *singer* of the Doors, that 'other' Jim Morrison:

> *Snakeskin jacket*
> *Indian eyes*
> *Brilliant hair*
>
> *He moves in disturbed*
> *Nile Insect*
> *Air*

(*NC*, p. 3)

In the earlier poems in *The New Creatures*, we are introduced to James Douglas Morrison, *the poet*. References abound to his clothes, 'Indian' visions, Alexandrine hair, and shamanic dance moves — it is a story about himself. We are also introduced to the poet's perception of his reader:

> *You parade thru the soft summer*
> *We watch your eager rifle decay*
> *Your wilderness*
> *Your teeming emptiness*

*Pale forests on verge of light
decline.*

*More of your miracles
More of your magic arms*

(*NC*, p. 3)

'You,' are the reader along for the journey; 'we' are the 'lords,' the poet speaks—enlightened ones, the ones who can see 'your wilderness' . . . America? He continues: 'You' are lost now; 'we' are still the ones who can see what the reader cannot. Morrison invites us into his world, but the reader is always kept at 'arm's' length. 'Eager Rifle Decay' is a possible reference to the mindless use of violence by people who are not 'Lords' (enlightened). Further, it could be read as representing the decline (decay) of Western civilisation.

In the next section of the poem, we are introduced to the state of the world and its inhabitants — disease, despair, images of torture, and the ominous presence of death always lurking in the background. A strange exotic world is revealed, with rites and customs straight out of Frazer's *The Golden Bough*:[4]

> *Bitter grazing in sick pastures
> Animal sadness & the daybed
> Whipping.
> Iron curtains pried open.
> The elaborate sun implies
> dust, knives, voices.
> Call out of the Wilderness*

> *Call out of fever, receiving*
> *the wet dreams of an Aztec King.*
>
> (*NC,* p. 4)

The 'elaborate' sun is elaborate in its context; the 'iron curtain' forcibly opened reveals war, communism, Stalinist tyranny, etc. The 'sun' could be a reference to the East, the land of the rising sun (also the name of a city in Ohio); its place in the wilderness, 'implies' ancient and customary qualities of meaning. The Aztec King brings a whole new dimension and significance to the sun as the ancient Mayans used the blood of human sacrifices to strengthen the daily journey of the sun across the sky.[5]

The following poem (VII) from *The New Creatures*, exemplifies the remainder of the poems in this group section (i.e., *The NC*):

> *Lizard woman*
> *w/ your insect eyes*
> *w/ your wild surprise.*
> *Warm daughter of silence.*
> *Venom.*
> *Turn your back w/ a slither of moaning*
> *wisdom.*
> *The unblinking blind eyes*
> *behind walls new histories rise*
> *and wake growling & whining*
> *the weird dawn of dreams.*
> *Dogs lie sleeping.*
> *The wolf howls.*
> *A creature lives out the war.*

A forest.
A rustle of cut words, choking
river.

(*NC*, p. 6)

This poem, simply titled 'VII,' is the seventh in a series of eight poems, which form the main section of 'The New Creatures (To Pamela Susan).' A series of interconnected free-verse stanzas form the remainder of the *NC* and don't appear to be linked to the first eight poems. The eight poems appear to be unified as a series, forming one larger work. The poems and vignettes that accompany this first section are linked in motif but appear to be ephemeral (to the first part), apart from the sections titled I-III and beginning with the line 'The soft parade has now begun…' The poems are aphoristic, almost haikuish [sic] stanzas, and appear at first glance somewhat random.

Upon closer reading, a transition seems to take place with a shift in time to the modern, from the more mythological and ancient setting of the first group of poems, to the more chaotic and discordant themes of race, war and cultural disquiet. Like the remainder of the poem/s, the verse above suggests that history is shaped by myth as much it is by tradition and events. History is made contextual, and always with recourse to myth, ritual and prophecy (in Morrison's world).

The first quatrain of 'VII' directly addresses the ideal (mythological) woman and suggests that the deity-like 'Lizard woman' would turn her back on the discord of her modern counterparts (i.e., outlined in the second quatrain). The 'wisdom' is present in the more natural and god-like response of the snake-like lizard woman as she turns her back, unimpressed and wise. She knows that such trifles of human concern are pointless and do nothing to counter the fate of humanity, let alone the ideal female figure who has attained ascendance in her acceptance of her place in myth and social standing.

Every line is imbued with mystery and suggestion. 'Behind walls new histories rise…' – political decisions made in locked rooms whose outcomes ultimately lead to war, foretold by prophecy (Nostradamus, Cayce, etc.) – '…wake growling & whining the weird dawn of dreams.'

Again, the preceding line, '[t]he unblinking blind eyes,' implies both literal and mythical meaning with a nod to the blind seer, Tiresias.[6]

Highly symbolic and ambiguous, the histories which 'rise' seem to be offspring, almost zombie-like and animalistic. Morrison's preoccupation with word-play and double entendre is fairly obviously in use throughout the verse.

The obvious reference to the notion of 'let sleeping dogs lie,' present in the line 'Dogs lie sleeping,' reinforces the idea that things should be left as they are in order to avoid war (literal and cultural). The alpha-male/war is represented by the howling wolf, who is also a sacred and symbolic idealised representation of (human) nature, that will always howl, no matter what happens in 'the forest.' The 'creature [who] lives out the war' is the Lizard woman, who in her sage wisdom has prophetically realised the futility of cultural and political battles and retreated back into the sanctuary of the mythological forest (nature).

The 'rustle of cut words, choking river' symbolises speech (words) as detritus, falling like leaves into the river only to be deathly obstacles to the flow of human existence as symbolised by the river motif. All the various factions and ideologies and their respective manifestoes only serve to 'rustle' the true nature of things (as represented by the forest), but are metaphorically cut-down and clog the sacred river of life.[7]

Once again, this verse represents Morrison's veneration of women as sacred or mystical beings, while the ambiguity suggests that the 'woman' is reptilian or even dog-like and therefore a counterpart to 'The Lizard King.' A new creature, possibly representative of the new left, feminism ('born of silence,' from generations of women who were taught that their place is 'to be seen and not heard') stands next to freedom (of speech, democracy etc.) and the anti-war movement.

In these verses, we see the central motifs of Morrison's poetic paraded before us: women, death, history, transformative parahumans (part animal/part human) war, dreams and visions – synonymous with Morrison and the Romantic tradition (e.g. Blake, Baudelaire, and to some degree Rimbaud).

Something else to bear in mind when interpreting Morrison's poetry is the constant allusion to poetical tradition and technique. In this instance, the last quatrain (*NC*, VII) seems to stand alone. Given that

Morrison was quite taken with the Surrealists and the Beats, who often used the "cut-up" technique (taking text and randomly 'cutting' sections and mixing them randomly etc.) – check out the last two lines of this stanza: 'A rustle of cut words...' It may not mean anything in the context of the rest of the poem, but an awareness of this tendency of Morrison's to use such devices (i.e. literary and technical) is important in understanding why he structures his verse the way it is.

If he can work multiple meaning and allusion into a line of poetry, chances are *he will* employ layering techniques to advance the depth of meaning and the power of the metaphor. As can be seen from this close reading, the interpretation of implied meaning through metaphor, symbolism, allusion and reference is limited only by the lengths the critic is willing to take with an analysis of Morrison's poetry.

The poems in *The New Creatures* and his other works are filled with allusion and symbolism that often borders on the surreal. Some of the poems and the smaller verses read like vignettes or thoughts and, as stated above, appear to employ literary techniques like the 'cut-up'[8] technique pioneered by the Dadaists and championed by contemporaries of Morrison's such as William S Burroughs and Brion Gysin. The following poem is a good example of these poetic devices that Morrison employs:

> *He spoke to me. He frightened*
> *me w / laughter. He took*

> *my hand, & led me past*
> *silence into cool whispered*
> *Bells.*
>
> *A file of young people*
> *going thru a small woods*

(*NC*, 14)

As a stand-alone piece this is obviously very ambiguous. The astute reader may or may not find a reference to Dante's inferno, with the character being led into the dark woods by a maniacal Virgil-like poet figure. Apparently random stanzas of this sort, are common throughout Morrison's poetic oeuvre and are hurdles by which critics and readers alike must cross if they are to interpret the meaning of the poems.

As with other similar poems, they appear nonsensical and surreal, but when read in the context of the larger body of work they start to make sense. Contextually, Morrison's notion of the 'lords' gives us a clue as to the central motif – the main characteristic of the Nietzschean-type 'Lord' being instinct.

The way the first-person character is being 'led' implies that the character has the instinctual nature of a female. Is it really a female being led into the woods by some potentially violent Charles Manson/Svengali/Lord type of figure? Is this interpretation worth making and is it correct?

Possibly so, but when read in the context of the following poem it becomes apparent that the implication is confirmed.

> *I don't dig what they did*
> *to that girl*
> *Mercy pack*
> *Wild song they sing*
> *As they chop her hands*
> *Nailed to a ghost*
> *Tree*

(*NC*, 15)

This verse-section (as part of the overall poem), possibly refers to an incident where a girl was pack-raped by a group of bikers in the 1960s, or to another incident where a young black-girl was violently raped and murdered by Ku Klux Klan members around the same period. Both were highly publicised cases at the time and maybe that is what he's mythologizing in this instance?

The technique of taking a modern historical occurrence and combining it with a literary/mythological event (i.e. the scene from Dante's *Inferno*) is prevalent throughout Morrison's writing. Once again, also notice the juxtaposition of the verse – it seems to be 'cut-up,' as indicated by the placement of punctuation and the use of capitalisation and disparate elements.

The characters of the poems are 'creatures' of a nightmarish world, their populations heavily concentrated in the cities. It is only upon realising that the creatures are meant to be us (modern humans), that the fragments of society, held up to us as a mirror of ourselves through the experience of the author, become familiar.

Gaze Into The Abyss

Robert Duncan, a poet from Morrison's era, in a passage reminiscent of Morrison's credo of 'wake up' and the paradoxical consequence of his (Morrison's) beliefs, perhaps best sums up the poet's meaning and reason for creating such a world:

> It is in the dream itself that we seem entirely creatures, without imagination, as if moved by a plot or myth told by a story-teller who is not ourselves. Wandering and wondering in a foreign land or struggling in the meshes of a nightmare, we cannot escape the compelling terms of the dream unless we wake, anymore than we can escape the terms of our living reality unless we die.[9]

Later in his life, as a more mature and serious writer, Morrison attempted to awaken from his own 'living reality.' One of the reason for doing so was that he had become very aware of the naïveté of his early work. He reflects on the significance of some of his early ideas and acknowledges the limits of his experience and youthful literary talents, in terms of an expression of his life, art, and as a 'prophetic' poet:

> I think in art, but especially in films, people are trying to confirm their own existence. Somehow things seem more real if they can be photographed and you can create a semblance of life on the screen. But those little aphorisms that make up most of *The Lords* — if I could have said it any other way, I would have. They tend to be mulled

over. I take a few seriously. I did most of that book when I was at the film school at UCLA. It was really a thesis on film [a]esthetics. I wasn't able to make films then, so all I was able to do was think about them and write about them, and it probably reflects a lot of that. A lot of passages in it — for example about shamanism — turned out to be very prophetic several years later because I had no idea when I was writing that, that I'd be doing just that.[10]

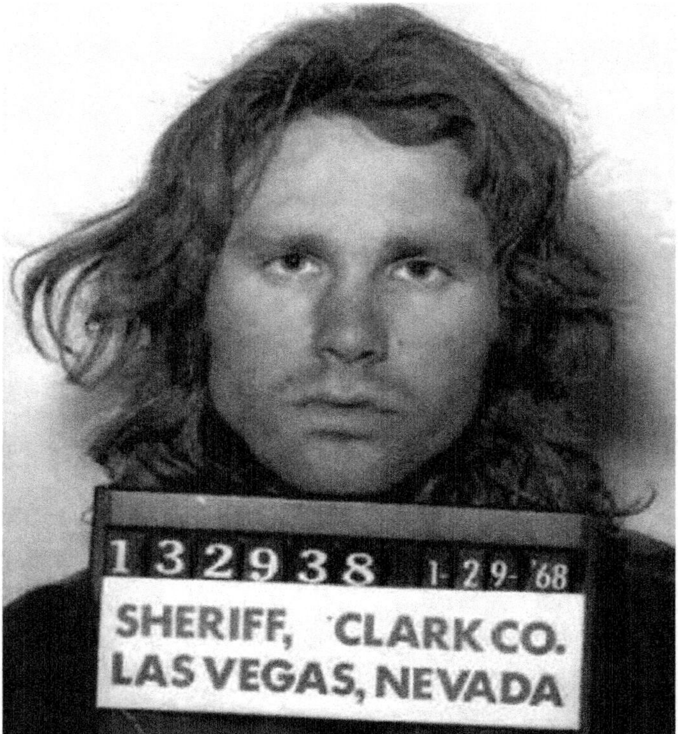
132938 1-29-'68
SHERIFF, CLARK CO.
LAS VEGAS, NEVADA

V. Shamanism, Ideals, & Ritual

> *'Life lived in the absence of the psychedelic experience that primordial shamanism is based on is life trivialized, life denied, life enslaved to the ego.'*
>
> Terence McKenna

After the publication of Aldous Huxley's *The Doors of Perception* and *Heaven and Hell*[1], an increase in the availability of recreational drugs and the popularity of Blake's poetry, radical experimentation by poets and artists flourished in the '60s. Morrison, equally influenced by these ideas, applied them to his life, by romantically drawing on Blake's dictum that 'the road of excess leads to the palace of wisdom.' He inundated his senses with a barrage of stimulants in order to invoke the 'shaman's' vision — an aspect of Morrison's aesthetic idealisation of the role of the poet-performer.

His notion of the shaman was an integral aspect of his philosophy in regard to the way he lived his life and how he used poetry and performance to 'break on through.' For Morrison, the shaman wasn't only an ideal representation of the poet/performer elevated to mystical heights, it was a connection to the rituals and beliefs of the first nation tribes of pre-European America. His affinity with native American culture is closely related to his first real experience with death and subsequent visionary experience:

> . . . the first time I discovered death - me and my mother and father [. . .] and my grandmother and grandfather, were driving through the desert at dawn . . . and a truckload of Indian workers had either hit another car or I don't know what happened, but there were Indians scattered all over the highway; bleeding to death [. . .] And it's my first reaction to death. I must have been about four or five [. . .] the reaction I get now thinking back, looking back, is that possibly, the soul of one of those Indians, maybe several of them, just ran over and jumped into my brain [. . .] that was the first time I tasted fear. And like this is a projection from a long way back, but i do think that, at that moment, the soul of the ghosts of those dead Indians, maybe one or two of 'em, were just run-in around freaking out, and just leaped into my soul, and I was like a sponge ready to just sit there and absorb it. It's not a ghost story man, it's something that really means something to me.[2]

Combined with the influence of Blake's messianic path of knowledge, Morrison managed to give his quest a distinctive American flavour with the use of indigenous folklore and cultural symbolism. Believing he was directly linked with the indigenous peoples of the Americas, he saw himself as a poet in terms of a lineage of unity of location and practice:

> *Like our ancestors*
> *The Indians*
> *We share a fear of sex*
> *excessive lamentation for the dead*
> *& an abiding interest in dreams & visions*
>
> (*W*, p. 71)

However, Morrison's notion of what constituted the role of a shaman, somewhat differed from that of the spiritual practices of native American cultures who never ascribed the word 'shaman' to any of their rites or religious/spiritual leaders. Morrison's concept is more of an over-arching understanding of the shaman's role, not necessarily distinct to indigenous American cultural practice but, rather, ascribed to it. In *Shamanism: Archaic Techniques of Ecstasy*,[3] Mircea Eliade, a leading historian of religious experience, defines shamanism as:

> . . . a technique of religious ecstasy. Shamanism encompasses the premise that shamans are intermediaries or messengers between the human world and the spirit worlds. Shamans are said to treat ailments/illness by mending the soul. Alleviating traumas affecting the soul/spirit restores the physical body of the individual to balance and wholeness. The shaman also enters supernatural

realms or dimensions to obtain solutions to problems afflicting the community. Shamans may visit other worlds/dimensions to bring guidance to misguided souls and to ameliorate illnesses of the human soul caused by foreign elements. The shaman operates primarily within the spiritual world, which in turn affects the human world. The restoration of balance results in the elimination of the ailment.[4]

Morrison's conception of the shaman was more of a conflagration of historical records (such as Eliade's) of the common practices of ethnic mystics and tribal leaders, combined with the practice of the 'derangement of the senses' (ala Rimbaud and Blake) in order to experience visions and knowledge of 'the other side':

The Shaman . . . was a man who would intoxicate himself. See, he was probably already an . . . unusual individual. And, he would put himself into a trance by dancing, whirling around, drinking, taking drugs -- however [he could]. Then, he would go on a mental travel and . . . describe his journey to the rest of the tribe.[5]

And yet, despite what Morrison describes above, his ideal is inescapably imbued with contemporary white-American values and beliefs, which did more to invoke the struggle of good and evil than dispel it with any transcendental magical rite. His combination of traditional shamanic rites with Blakean dictums of knowledge by excess, were a recipe for self-destruction and characteristic wild swings between good and downright obscure poetry.

Despite his own misadventures with his concept of the role of poet/performer as shaman, Morrison was all too aware of the dangers of staring into the abyss via a 'prolonged derangement of the senses.' Experiential knowledge of the sort proposed by Morrison required potential sacrifice; both of sanity and, ultimately, the physical body:

> In the séance, the shaman led. A sensuous panic, deliberately evoked through drugs, chants, dancing, hurls the shaman into trance. Changed voice, convulsive movement. He acts like a madman.
>
> (*L*, p.24)

Morrison's interest in the shaman was common amongst other poets of the time as well, but each had different views that represented an era of diverse, often 'exotic' and factitious beliefs. For example, Jerome Rothenberg, a poet and critic associated with 'deep-image'[6] verse in the '60s and '70s, encouraged a shamanistic type of poetry, where primitive song takes precedence over received forms of English letters. However, Rothenberg did not want to appropriate 'shamanship,' and what he called the 'fable of ascendancy,' nor did he want to have much to do with people who did:

> *the old people*

> *ghosts will arise anew*
> *in phantom cities*
> *they will drive caravans across the land*
> *bare chested gods*
> *of neither morning*
> *shaman serpent in thy final kingdom leave*
> *my house in peace* [7]

In this poem, characteristically similar to Morrison's work, but different in ideas, Rothenberg emphasises the resigned tone of the mature realist, a tone that Morrison himself would adopt in his later verse. Instead, in his earlier writings, Morrison's idea of the shamanic vision is the antithesis of Rothenberg's:

> *The dark girl begins to bleed.*
> *It's Catholic heaven. I have an*
> *ancient Indian crucifix around*
> *my neck. My chest is hard*
> *& brown. Lying on stained &*
> *wretched sheets w/ a bleeding Virgin.*
> *We could plan a murder, or*
> *Start a religion.*
>
> (*AN*, p. 124)

Aside from shamanism, Rothenberg also summed up nicely, in a letter to Robert Creeley (another well-known American poet), the principles of deep image. As can be seen below, these principles are applicable to Morrison's sense of poetic style and vision as a poet transitioning from the influence of the modern (in particular, romantic avant-gardism) to the more 'postmodern' sensibility and influence of his peers and cultural experience:

> The poem is the record of a movement from perception to vision.
> Poetic form is the pattern of that movement through space and time.
> The deep image is the content of vision emerging in the poem.
> The vehicle of movement is imagination.
> The condition of movement is freedom.[8]

The underlying idea that perception is malleable and that consciousness can be expanded, is a central tenet of the Beat poets as well as Morrison. The idea was made explicit in the French poet Rimbaud's Blakean 'derangement of the senses' and also in Baudelaire's 'Le Voyage'; that is, the 'fire that burns our brains, to plunge into the depths of the abyss, Hell or Heaven . . . [t]o the depths of the unknown to find something *new*.'[9] Rimbaud's proclamations in his 1871 letter to Paul Demeny, would ultimately prove the most influential to Morrison's aesthetic sensibility and his notion of himself as poet seer:

> The first study of the man who wants to be a poet in the knowledge of himself, complete. He looks for his soul, inspects it, tests it, learns it. As soon as he knows it, he must cultivate it! It seems simple: in every mind a natural development takes place; so many *egoists* call themselves authors, there are many others who attribute their intellectual progress to themselves! — But the soul must be made

monstrous: in the fashion of the comprachicos ['kidnappers of children who mutilate them in order to exhibit them as monsters'], if you will! Imagine a man implanting and cultivating warts on his face.

I say one must be a *seer*, make oneself a *seer*.

The poet makes himself a *seer* by a long, gigantic and rational *derangement of all the senses*. All forms of love, suffering, and madness. He searches himself. He exhausts all poisons in himself and keeps only their quintessence. Unspeakable torture where he needs all his faith, all his superhuman strength, where he becomes among all men the great patient, the great criminal, the one accursed — and the supreme Scholar! — Because he reaches the *unknown*! Since he cultivated his soul, rich already, more than any man! He reaches the unknown, and when, bewildered, he ends by losing the intelligence of his visions, he has seen them. Let him die as he leaps through unheard of and unnameable things: other horrible workers will come; they will begin from the horizons where the other one collapsed![10]

Rimbaud's views, combined with Morrison's knowledge of shamanic rituals and philosophical/mythological dogma, were the main ingredients that formulated his prescription for experience and what he thought would be the road to an expanded consciousness. The prospect of gaining knowledge by sexual and hedonistic excess would have, of course, held great appeal for Morrison as a transformative sensory experience :

By listening to your body – opening up your senses, Blake said that the body was the soul's prison unless the five senses are fully developed and open. He considered the senses the 'windows of the soul.' When sex involves all the senses intensely, it can be like a mystical experience . . . If you reject your body, it becomes your prison cell. It's a paradox — to transcend the limitations of the body, you have to immerse yourself in it — you have to be totally open to your senses.[11]

In addition, in relation to his stage performances with The Doors, Morrison emphasises the transcendent quality of his ethos — the constant search for revelation and transformation. The paragraph below reveals that his goal as a performer is closely aligned with his personal ethos and mission as a poet:

It's a search, an opening of one door after another. Our work, our performing, is a striving for a metamorphosis. Right now, we're more interested in the dark side of life, the evil thing, the night time. But through our music, we're striving, trying to break through to a cleaner, freer realm. Our music and personalities as seen in the performance are still in a state of chaos and disorder, with maybe an element of purity just showing. Lately, when we've appeared in concert, it's started to merge.[12]

More in line with Blake and Nietzsche's aesthetic and messianic path of knowledge, Morrison manages to give his quest a distinctive flavour with the use and influence of indigenous folklore, mystical ritual and cultural symbolism — characteristics that ultimately make it distinctly American.

Morrison acknowledged he was a product and the embodiment of a violent age; essentially, he had reached a cross-roads of self-realisation. Within his poetry, we find suggestion that Morrison desired the death of all he had come to represent. A later poem such as 'Hurricane and Eclipse' (from his posthumously published *Notebook Poems*) epitomises this weariness and self-flagellation:

> *I wish a storm would*
> *come & blow this shit*
> *away. Or a bomb to*
> *burn the Town & scour*
> *the sea. I wish clean*
> *death would come to me.*

(*AN*, p. 185)

When he states in his poetry his wish to die; it is hard to see it as merely a desire to die figuratively. Rather, there is a sense that it is somehow the shamanistic poet's duty to sacrifice the self, in order to save the tribe. As he had said in an interview, the whole 'death trip' was not entirely of his own making, although he wore the role of martyr like a crown:

I'm not sure it's salvation that people are after, or want me to lead them to. The shaman is a healer — like the witch-doctor. I don't see people turning to me for that. I don't see myself as a saviour . . . The shaman is similar to the scapegoat. I see the role of the artist as shaman and scapegoat. People project their fantasies onto him and their fantasies come alive. People can destroy their fantasies by destroying him [the poet/shaman]. I obey the impulses everyone has, but won't admit to. By attacking me, punishing me, they can feel relieved of those impulses. [13]

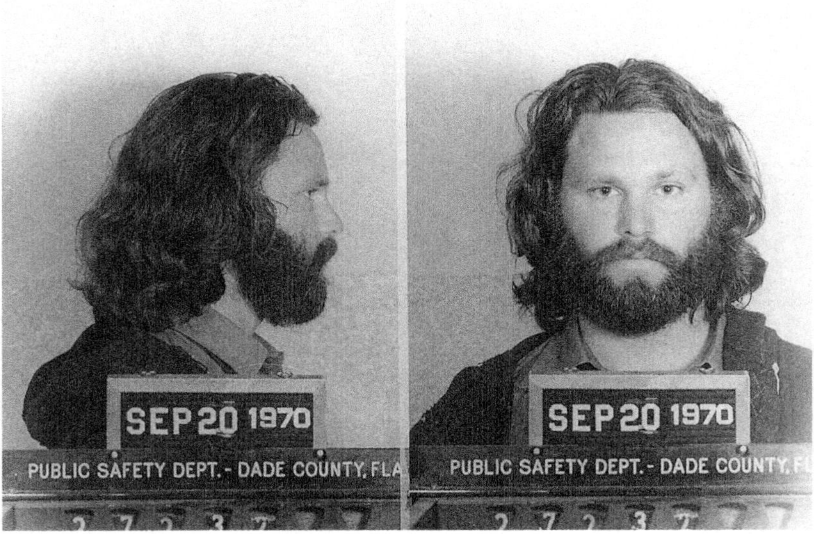
SEP 20 1970
PUBLIC SAFETY DEPT. - DADE COUNTY, FLA
SEP 20 1970
PUBLIC SAFETY DEPT. - DADE COUNTY, FL

VI. The Influence of Style

> *'What is a poet? An unhappy man who hides deep anguish in his heart, but whose lips are so formed that when the sigh and cry pass through them, it sounds like lovely music... And people flock around the poet and say: 'Sing again soon' — that is, 'May new sufferings torment your soul but your lips be fashioned as before, for the cry would only frighten us, but the music, that is blissful.'*

Soren Kierkegaard

In his book, *The Living Theatre, Art, Exile, and Outrage*,[1] John Tytell recalls Morrison and poet-friend Michael McClure participating in performances of *Paradise Now* with 'The Living Theatre' company. He also recalls how Morrison offered financial aid to the theatre troupe such was his commitment to the art. Tytell offers an important insight into Morrison's political and aesthetic beliefs and also his loyalty and support of fellow artists:

VI. The Influence of Style

> Morrison — who had read Artaud and Ginsberg in college — saw himself as a revolutionary figure. Agreeing that repression was the chief social evil in America and the cause of a general pathology, he was typical of the sectors of support The Living Theatre had received in America. His long improvisational song 'When the Music's Over' was a basic statement of apocalypse. Another of his songs proclaims, as in *Paradise Now*, 'we want the world and we want it now.' Morrison had seen every performance in Los Angeles and followed the company up to San Francisco.[2]

Tytell's portrayal of Morrison as a revolutionary figure aligned with the likes of Artaud and Ginsberg, and his suggestion that Morrison had a doomed ('apocalyptic') view of an oppressive American society, simplifies Morrison's philosophy and assumes that his song lyrics were the totality of his world-view. Morrison's poetry, however, while displaying a penchant for shocking imagery, avant-garde style and taboo subject matter, also reveals the presence of a cultured mind whose philosophy, while not afraid to tackle the darker aspects of humanity, shows a profound interest in humanism and spirituality.

The distinction between Morrison's performance and poetry, while closely aligned, is nonetheless apparent in the more rigorous and well-defined philosophical imperative that can be found in his poetry. While the structure, immediacy and thematic similarities of Morrison's verse to the likes of Artaud's and Ginsberg's can be seen, there are subtle but distinctive

VI. The Influence of Style

aspects that distinguish Morrison's *concerns* from that of other poets.

The founder of the Theatre-of-Cruelty, Antonin Artaud, described the motifs of his plays in his manifesto *Theatre and Cruelty*, as 'eroticism, savagery, bloodlust, a thirst for violence, an obsession with horror, collapse of moral values, social hypocrisy, lies, sadism, the plague, disease and depravity' amongst other things.[3] Despite the prevalence of similar themes, motifs and style, Morrison distinguishes himself from Artaud's despondency with a continual recourse to diametric expressions of freedom, love, friendship, nature and spiritual awakening.

The essence of Morrison's poetry resonates, in an exploratory sense, with the journey of self-discovery as both a society (American) and as individuals, especially as it relates to good and evil and to the relation between the natural (wilderness, instinct, spirit) and the artificial (the city, social structure, etc.). The purpose of his exploration was resolutely tied to his conception of the role of poet as seer and the exposition of experiential truth. In an interview, Morrison flippantly dismisses his quest as mere curiosity:

> Let's just say I was testing the bounds of reality. I was curious to see what would happen. That's all it was: curiosity.[4]

Despite his posturing for journalists, his commitment to ideas and art was anything but trivial. As

VI. The Influence of Style

Tytell recollects, Morrison had an understanding of Antonin Artaud's theoretical ideas, and went to performances by The Living Theatre Company, which in turn informed his own performances with The Doors. His commitment to his own art and his constant reference to art and artists that he admired (including musicians, thespians and, of course, poets and writers), showed that art, especially music and poetry, were core values in his life.

Influence can be found in most aspects of Morrison's work, similar to most poets who write within a traditional canon. Other than allusion, imitation and theme, his work finds similarities with others in a stylistically aesthetic sensibility.

For example, the influence of Artaud the poet on Morrison's verse style is evident when reading both of the authors' works side-by-side. Artaud's poetry is very similar in the free-verse form, style and subject matter, especially the way in which he juxtaposes violent imagery with archetypal symbols to invoke a nightmarish sense of reality. In a remarkable passage where Artaud describes what surrealism means to him, we find an almost accurate description of Morrison's perception of art and performance:

> Surrealism was never anything else than a new sort of magic to me. Imagination and dreams, all this intensive freeing of the unconscious whose aim was that those things the soul is accustomed to hiding should *break through* [italics mine], and must of necessity usher in a profound transformation in the scale of appearances, in the value of meanings and

VI. The Influence of Style

creative symbolism. Concrete matter entirely changes its garb, its shell and no longer applies to the same mental gestures. The beyond, the unseen, reject reality. The world collapses. Then we can start examining our illusions and stop pretending.[5]

The similarities to Morrison's own aesthetic are evident in the following passage quoted from *The Doors: The Illustrated History*:

I offer images — I conjure memories of freedom that can still be reached — like The Doors, right? But we can only open the doors — we can't drag people through. I can't free them unless they want to be free— more than anything else . . . Maybe primitive people have less bullshit to let go of, to give up. A person has to be willing to give up everything — not just wealth. All the bullshit he's been taught — all society brainwashing. You have to let go of all that to get to the other side. Most people aren't willing to do that.[6]

Allan Ginsberg's use of Whitman's epigraph, preceding his (Ginsberg's) famous poem *Howl*, is used in the same sense as Morrison's own conception of the 'doors':

Unscrew the locks from the doors!
Unscrew the doors themselves from their jambs!

Walt Whitman's *Leaves of Grass* — his declaration

VI. The Influence of Style

of the sacred self, an egalitarian America, and the immortality of the soul — was the precursor model for the American poet's characteristic sense of duty to expand their own, and their nation's, consciousness. Morrison possibly took his cue by way of Ginsberg's adoption of Whitman's symbolic poetic principle, as much as he did from Blake's dictum in 'The Marriage of Heaven and Hell' that reads: 'if the doors of perception were cleansed everything would appear to man as it is, infinite.'[7]

Morrison's use of symbolism and analogy, that had deep literary connections and links to mythological and psychological archetypes, was a significant characteristic of his poetry. The 'door' as the title of his band, and as the symbol of Morrison's own search for enlightenment, was evidence of his knowledge and use of symbolism, but also of his awareness of a tradition in literary sigils and their potential for reference to a particular canonical lineage.

In this regard, Morrison's adaptation and use of these literary devices reveals a complexity of meaning and a depth of allusion that not only adds to the overall effect and significance of his poetry, but also aligns it with the (American) Romantic Visionary tradition.

Morrison's writing is a reflection of his own world: a journey into the unknown, an extension of the heroic rebel's philosophy (re. Joseph Campbell's *Hero of a Thousand Faces*) to 'break on through to the other side,' where everything is spontaneous and unassured, apart

VI. The Influence of Style

from immortality. This world is a creative amalgam of influence, ideas, and experience, all of which contribute to Morrisons's poetical conception of the universe.

His work is a quest, not so much into the world of the unknown realms or spirituality, but rather a psychological immersion in his own being, a search for the essence of the individual 'self' and of the nation:

> America was conceived in violence. Americans are attracted to violence. They attach themselves to processed violence, out of cans. They're TV-hypnotised — TV is the invisible protective shield against bare reality. Twentieth-century culture's disease is the inability to feel their reality. People cluster to TV, soap operas, movies, theatre, pop idols, and they have wild emotion over symbols. But in the reality of their own lives, they're emotionally dead . . . we fear violence less than our own feelings. Personal, private, solitary pain is more terrifying than what anyone else can inflict.[8]

Eliot's free-verse pastiche style of *The Waste Land*, combined with Ginsberg's apocalyptic tone and gritty perception of 'America' in *Howl*, provide the structural models for Morrison's longer poems such as 'American Prayer,' which also focuses on aspects of society in terms of a psychological landscape, and its imperfections. The poems can be read literally, with the effect being a sense of malaise or confusion. At times the poems are almost journalistic descriptions of a certain

VI. The Influence of Style

time and place, albeit a heavily symbolic and analogous one.

Read figuratively, or metaphorically, Morrison's 'better' poems take on a multi-layered depth filled with allusion, imagery, mood, and meaning that can be interpreted as either quite sublime or disconcerting. Perhaps the most difficult aspect of Morrison's poetry is that, at times, the verse appears fragmented and too freely associative; yet the reader must persevere, while not forgetting the chaotic and experimental age in which it was written and intended to translate.

Morrison chooses androgynous symbols and metaphorical figures to convey the mutability and temporality of his era, as in the lyrics of his song 'Riders on the Storm' from *LA Woman*, the last album he made with The Doors. 'Riders on the Storm' is a metaphor for those, such as the character of the 'lord' or Nietzsche's ubermensch, who are gods in their own right, riding the storm of violent experience and tempestuous forays into evil.

It is also a literary allusion to two particular poems by English and American romantic poets whose lives were similar as were the style and subject of their verse. William Cowper's hymnal poem 'God Moves in a Mysterious Way,' calls to saints to trust the storm, for it is of God's making, and it is he who 'rides upon the storm':

> *God moves in a mysterious way*
> *His wonders to perform;*
> *He plants his footsteps in the sea,*
> *And rides upon the storm.*[9]

VI. The Influence of Style

The other reference is to the poem 'Praise for an Urn' by Hart Crane, the wildly romantic American poet who inspired modern poets such as the Beats with his lust for life and experience, and his ultimate poetical act of suicide. This act of self-destruction, brought about no-doubt by his alcoholism, depression and confused sexuality, assured Crane's position as a tragic and sacrificial poet who sacrificed everything, seemingly, for his art.

'Praise for an Urn' is a poem full of metaphorical sentiment, suitable as a eulogy of sorts, for a dead 'friend' who is about to be cremated. Cowper's depiction of God as a natural entity becomes something different for Crane. The 'riders' are the fragile words and thoughts that ride the tumultuous storms of the mind and emotions.

> *His thoughts, delivered to me*
> *From the white coverlet and pillow,*
> *I see now, were inheritances —*
> *Delicate riders of the storm.* [10]

The words for the poem within the poem are 'inherited' from the person whose epitaph he writes. Like Morrison's later poems, they are personal moments and thoughts shared from someone whose mind was in turmoil, who perhaps in hindsight may have been whispering for help. Aware that those words, about to be cast into the crematorium with his friend's corpse, have a bittersweet profundity hard to match in other poetry are, he realises, 'no trophies of the sun.'

Morrison's use of 'riders *on* the storm' is different

VI. The Influence of Style

again in its implications, but shows an awareness of a romantic motif and subsequent tradition. His 'rider' is the outsider figure of the poet, the wanderer, the killer: 'like a dog without a bone / an actor out on loan,' unlike the more metaphysically romantic version of Cowper and Crane's making. Morrison's version of the rider is more like Stephen Crane's 'Rider' from *The Black Riders & Other Lines* (1895)

> *Black riders came from the sea.*
> *There was clang and clang of spear and*
>   *shield,*
> *And clash and clash of hoof and heel,*
> *Wild shouts and the wave of hair*
> *In the rush upon the wind:*
> *Thus the ride of sin.*

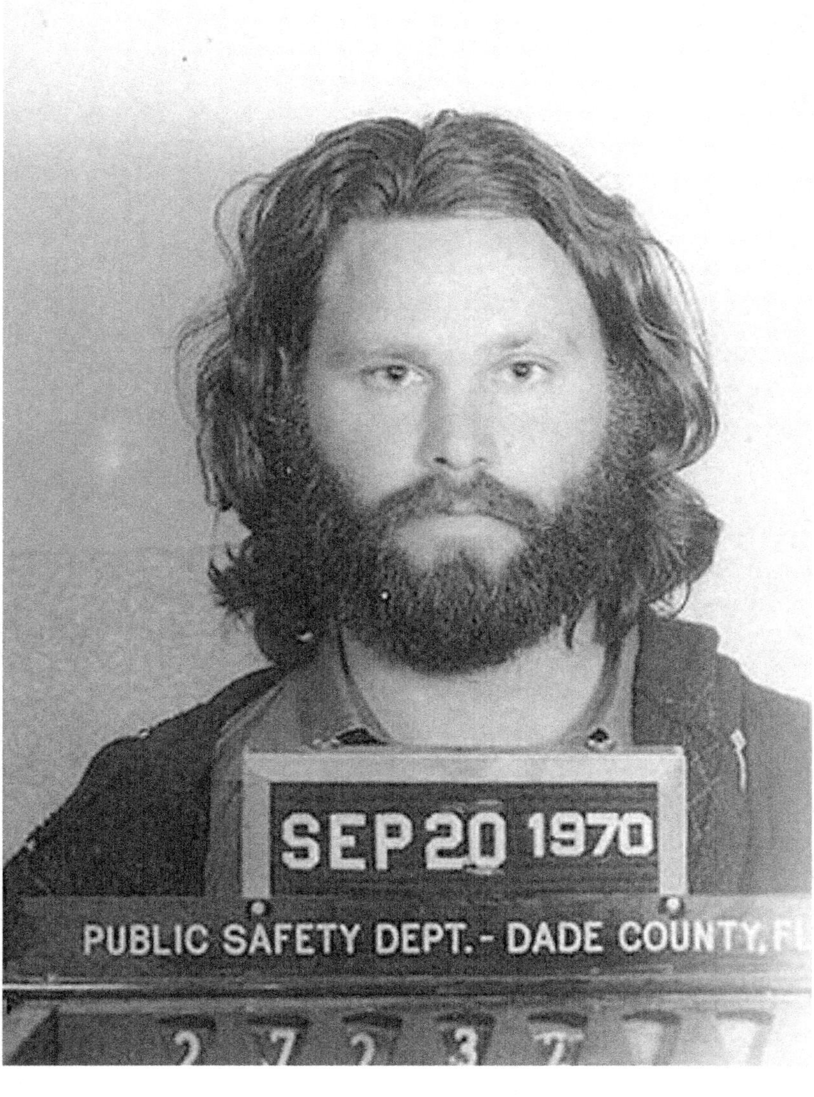
SEP 20 1970
PUBLIC SAFETY DEPT. - DADE COUNTY

VII. Conclusions

'The poet, therefore, is truly the thief of fire. He is responsible for humanity, for animals even; he will have to make sure his visions can be smelled, fondled, listened to; if what he brings back from beyond has form, he gives it form; if it has none, he gives it none. A language must be found...of the soul, for the soul and will, include everything: perfumes, sounds colors, thought grappling with thought.'

Arthur Rimbaud

James Douglas Morrison died in Paris on July 3, 1971, at the age of twenty-seven of a suspected drug overdose. Buried in the Pere-Lachaise cemetery, his grave sits alongside his literary heroes such as Oscar Wilde, Charles Baudelaire and Paul Verlaine.

Up until his death, Paris was an ideal world for Morrison. It was a place where Morrison's literary heroes originated from and gravitated to and a world that was compatible with his romantic notion of the

VII. Conclusions

poet. Ultimately, it was a place *to be* a poet, not a famous American pop icon.

Arguably, it was in Paris where Morrison wrote his most mature poetry — his verse bursting with American landscapes, history, philosophy, and literary allusion. However, also evident in the poems from this period, it was a time and place that made him feel isolated, depressed, and suicidal (see 'Notebook Poems' and 'Paris Journal,'). The outcome may have been different if Morrison had heeded the words of his favourite philosopher, Nietzsche, who said:

> ". . . as soon as ever a philosophy begins to believe in itself [. . .] It always creates the world in its own image; it cannot do otherwise; philosophy is this tyrannical impulse itself, the Will to Power, the will to 'creation of the world,' the will to the *causa prima*."[1]

As Morrison discovered, he could not escape the inevitable consequence of his own idealism.

Before he was a singer, Jim Morrison was a poet. He wrote poetry, published it, performed it on stage and lived as he thought a poet should live right to the end. Rather than merely write about experience, he would subject himself to that experience physically, psychologically, or chemically, before he wrote about it. Morrison proceeded to transform himself during his short life through a series of comprehensive rites of

VII. Conclusions

passage, much like the rituals of the American Indian Shaman.

He immersed himself in select works of literature and music, experimentation with different kinds of drugs and intoxicants, and physical forays into states of isolation and sexual encounter. Whatever the means, the crucial element was that whatever happened, the end-goal was always to have an intense experience that might induce a profound realisation of note. He methodically and consistently sought transformation and awakening through rituals and intoxication, and was honest enough to write it down for all to read:

> *Why do I drink?*
> *So that I can write poetry.*
> *Sometimes when it's all spun out*
> *and all that is ugly recedes*
> *into a deep sleep*
> *There is an awakening*
> *and all that remains is true.*
> *As the body is ravaged*
> *the spirit grows stronger.*
>
> *Forgive me Father for I know*
> *what I do.*
> *I want to hear the last Poem*
> *of the last Poet.*

(*W*, p. 119)

Morrison's conception of the role of the poet operates within the Romantic visionary tradition of

VII. Conclusions

the mythopoetic experience. He envisaged the primary role of the poet and the function of poetry as something mythological that could be manipulated and used to push the boundaries of convention and reality, in order to reveal insights and profundities. The concerts of the Doors were infamous for Jim's use of poetry to incite his audience into a state of reckless abandonment and transcendence.

Along with Morrison's use of the power of words to uplift people and to change lives, he also saw poetry as a means of continuing tradition, history, and art. Like William Blake, Carl Jung and Joseph Campbell, Morrison sees the poet as an archetypal heroic shaman who must confront the extremities of life in order to relay those experiences and discoveries back to the rest of humanity.

In order for the reader to see Morrison as a serious poet, with a clearly defined 'poetic,' we must read his work as poetry, rather than as a strange relic of a dead rock god. What follows is the prologue from Morrison's posthumous collection of poetry, *Wilderness*. From Morrison's own words we gain an insight into the importance of poetry and the role it played in both his performances and life:

> I'm kind of hooked to the game of art and literature; my heroes are artists and writers . . . I wrote a few poems, of course . . . real poetry doesn't say anything, it just ticks off the possibilities. Opens all doors. You can walk

VII. Conclusions

through any one that suits you . . . and that's why poetry appeals to me so much — because it's so eternal. As long as there are people, they can remember words and combinations of words. Nothing else can survive a holocaust but poetry and songs. No one can remember an entire novel . . . but so long as there are human beings, songs and poetry can continue. If my poetry aims to achieve anything, it's to deliver people from the limited ways in which they see and feel.

(*W*, p. 1- 2)

As can be seen, Morrison had a clearly defined aesthetic philosophy that would steer both his poetry and his performances (both onstage and off) throughout his life. Morrisons's adherence to the role of the poet and his production of poetry is, essentially, what makes Morrison a genuine poet.

What makes his best poetry good enough for inclusion in the American literary canon, is (in my view) the lingering effect that Morrison's poetry has on the reader. Not necessarily because of theme, or the significance of the words, the quality of the verse lies in the presentation of the poem as a total sum of all its parts. This quality can be found in the lingering strangeness of the effect, evoked by the visionary and surreal choice selection of words and symbols (combined with felicitous phrasing), in such a way that the poem 'speaks' to the reader.

It is precisely because of this 'quality' that causes readers and critics alike to either revere or loathe

VII. Conclusions

Morrison's poetry, due largely to the difficult and obscure nature of his verse. The reward for seeking the meaning of the words is the pay-off, if you will, for taking the time to *understand* the poetry on a deeper level, merely than reading and interpreting the text at a literal (and consequently) superficial level. Harold Bloom's words come to mind:

> One mark of originality that can win canonical status for a literary work is strangeness that we either never altogether assimilate, or that becomes such a given that we are blinded to its idiosyncrasies.[2]

Whether Morrison will ever be historically recognised as a poet worthy of canonical consideration, will depend largely on the passage of time and the amount and depth of critical attention applied to his poetry. A century from now, literary critics will look back on the twentieth century as a period of literary change and diversity.

Of course, the focus on various movements and figures of American literature in the '60s and '70s will be tempered by prejudices and preferences of those critics. This was an era of peak literary and social experiment and it would take a blind person to miss the significance of Jim Morrison to this crucial period in American cultural and literary history.

Morrison will stand out as a poet who represented a time when writers experimented with drugs, language, form, philosophy, music, theatre, and social

VII. Conclusions

revolution. It was a time similar to the Romantic era of the French Revolution, but a time and a set of characteristics distinctly relative to American culture in the '60s and '70s.

It should also be noted that the influence of the Romantic era and the characters of the poets themselves cannot be underestimated when analysing Morrison's poetry, especially in terms of the visionary nature of his work.

In one of the first studies to look critically at Morrison's poetry, Tony Magistrale points out that Morrison's poetry 'is as much a product of the Romantic poetic vein as William Blake, Walt Whitman, Edgar Allan Poe, Emily Dickinson and the French Symbolists were a century before him.

He also identifies Morrison's own quest for personal discovery and transformation as being closely aligned with these poets who were also preoccupied with 'breaking through to the other side . . . [to] discover what possible realms existed beyond the immediate and the material.' Morrison's best works, Magistrale suggests, 'defy quick dismissal.[3]

Heroes of Morrison's era will stand out via their narrative appeal to a future age when radicalism and confrontational behaviour will, perhaps, be of more interest than the typically conventional and canonically recognised poets. After all, Morrison's heroes such as Rimbaud, Artaud, Blake, and Nietzsche are examples of visionary artists and thinkers, deemed unworthy of the canon in their own age, now consid-

VII. Conclusions

ered exemplars of aesthetic style and genius in our time. Likewise, the same will be said of a poet like Morrison, whose work is at least, no less significant or deserving than minor canonical poets of his time.

If you can read Morrison's poetry with an open mind you will discover that the evidence of his ability can be found in his words. Having an awareness of his preoccupation with symbols, existential meaning, and philosophy, will also help the reader to navigate the labyrinthine nature of his poems.

With the passage of time and the continuing interest in his poetry, there is an increased awareness of the power of his lyrical skill, witnessed by the fact that more academic studies of his writing have emerged and other poets and artists have championed his poems.

As well-known American poet Michael McClure points out when discussing Morrison's *Lords & New Creatures*:

> . . . the poetry itself is adeptly twentieth century imagist poetry. It's almost mainstream, and it's good poetry, real fine poetry. It's as good as anybody of his generation; there's no better poet in Jim's generation.[4]

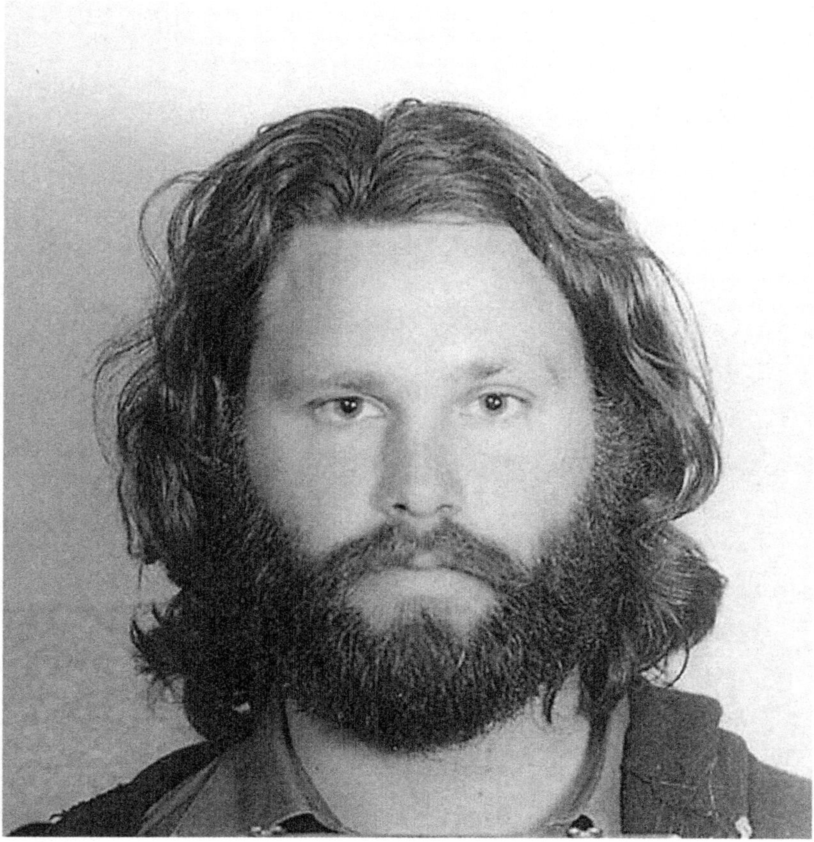

Appendix

Introduction

1. Hereafter, references to primary titles will be abbreviated within parentheses in indented quotes, as
    follows: *The Lords and New Creatures — LNC*, or alternatively as separate works — *L* or *NC*, *Wilderness —W*, and *The American Night —AN*.
2. *The American Night: The Writings of Jim Morrison* (Great Britain: Viking, 1991).
3. Ibid., *The American Night (*pg. 205).
4. Rothenberg & Quasha, *America: A prophecy* (1974), pp. xxx-xxxv.

I. Critiquing the Myth of Morrison

1. Wallace Fowlie, *Rimbaud & Jim Morrison: The Rebel as Poet* (1993).
2. Arthur Rimbaud, *Rimbaud: Complete Works, Selected Letters* (1966).
3. A Greek god, son of Zeus and Semele; his worship entered Greece from Thrace c.1000 BC. Originally a god of the fertility of nature, associated with wild and ecstatic religious rites, in later traditions he is a god of wine who loosens inhibitions and inspires creativity in music and poetry. Also called Bacchus. Source: https://en.oxforddictionaries.com/definition/dionysus
4. Fowlie (1993), p. 105.
5. Fowlie, *Rimbaud: The Myth of Childhood* (1946).
6. Jim Morrison, *The American Night: The Writings of Jim Morrison* (1991).
7. Fowlie (1993), p.97.

II. Motivation & Motif

1. Morrison, *The Lords and The New Creatures* (1985)
2. In Morrison's poetry, sex can be an act of love or an act of extreme violence/hate/rape, as in this stanza from *The New Creatures* (p 16):
    Hordes crawl & seep inside
    the walls. The streets

flow stone. Life goes
on absorbing war. Violence
kills the temple of no sex.

Violence begets violence – I interpret these lines to mean that while there is violence, sex will continue to propagate more life and therefore more violence – 'the temple of no sex', is to be worshipped because chastity is purity – a new plane of existence would occur with the death of the physical (i.e., without sex we would not exist physically) – it is an abstract line that can only be viewed abstractly. Once again, the ambiguity of this piece makes it appear purely metaphorical; however, in light of Morrison's interest in Eastern mysticism/mythology, it could also be read as a reference to the Buddhist view of chastity? Hard to say definitely.

3. John Tobler & Andrew Doe, *In Their Own Words: The Doors* (1988), p. 92
4. Ibid., p. 75.
5. This notion of Morrison's is also quite similar to Nietzsche's who, in his preface to *Twilight of the*

Idols, states that "in a wound there is the power to heal. A maxim . . . long been my motto: *Increscunt*

animi, virescit volnere virtus. ["Courage grows, strength is renewed through wounding."]
6. Tobler & Doe (1988), p. 75.
7. Charles Baudelaire, *Baudelaire: Selected Poems* (1995), p. 89.
8. Arthur Rimbaud, *Rimbaud: Poems* (1994), 'Parisian Orgy', p. 53.
9. Danny Sugerman, *The Doors: The Illustrated History* (1988), p. 188.
10. More of the more interesting aspects of Morrison's work is that whenever allusion or influence presents itself (for example, in his reimagining of Nietzsche's ideas), upon close reading I found that he would consistently engage with the concept (in an almost playful manner) by reversing the core principle or mutating it to effectively make it his own. In this regard, he seems to be using a technique similar to the 'cut-up technique' (or *découpé* in French), in which a written text is cut up (figuratively/literally) and rearranged to create a new text. The concept can be traced back to the Dadaists and Surrealists, but re-emerged in the late 1950s and early 1960s through the practice of writers such as William S. Burroughs, and artists like Brion Gysin.

III. Philosophy, Poetry, & America

1. Hopkins and Sugerman, *No One Here Gets Out Alive*, (1996), p. 17.

Appendix

2. John Densmore, *Riders on the Storm: My Life with Jim Morrison & the Doors* (1990), p. 3.
3. Ray Manzarek, *Light My Fire: My Life with the Doors* (1998), p. 350.
4. Sugerman (1988), p. 74.
5. Tobler & Doe (1988), p. 85
6. Morrison, (1991), pp. 116-191.
7. Ibid., pp. 193-204.
8. Philip Grundlehner, *The Poetry of Nietzsche* (1986), p.16.
9. Sugerman (1988), p. 161
10. Doe & Tobler, *In Their Own Words: The Doors* (Essex: Omnibus Press, 1988), p. 45
11.
12. Sugerman (1988), p. 122
13. Ibid., p. 160.
14. The death of Brian Jones was examined again in his later poem: 'Ode to LA While Thinking of Brian Jones, Deceased' - (*Wilderness*, pg. 128)

IV. Poetic & Poet

1. Doe & Tobler (1988), p. 85
2. *Wilderness: The Lost Writings of Jim Morrison* (London: Penguin Group, 1990, 'Introduction,' pg. 2.
3. Morrison (1991), pp. 3-9.
4. Sir James Frazer, *The Golden Bough: A Study in Magic & Religion* (1993). This book is central to
    Morrison's use of myth, mysticism, and symbol throughout his poetry.
5. Douglas J. Davies, *Death, Ritual, & Belief* (1997), 'Aztec Human Sacrifices,' p.76
6. Tiresias is an interesting and pivotal mythological figure for Morrison, whilst not being directly referenced, the blind prophet is present in many of his poems. The motifs and symbolism that pervade the legend of Tiresias are found everywhere throughout Morrison's work – snakes, prophets, sacrifice, gods, ambiguity, sexuality, death, the number 'seven', mysticism . . . the list goes on. From Wikipedia: *"In Greek mythology, Tiresias was a blind prophet of Apollo in Thebes, famous for clairvoyance and for being transformed into a woman for seven years. He was the son of the shepherd Everes and the nymph Chariclo. Tiresias participated fully in seven generations at Thebes, beginning as advisor to Cadmus himself . . . On Mount Cyllene in the Peloponnese, as Tiresias came upon a pair of copulating snakes, he hit the pair a smart blow with his stick. Hera was not pleased, and she punished Tiresias by transforming him into a woman. As a woman, Tiresias became a*

Appendix

priestess of Hera, married and had children, including Manto, who also possessed the gift of prophecy. According to some versions of the tale, Lady Tiresias was a prostitute of great renown. After seven years as a woman, Tiresias again found mating snakes; depending on the myth, either she made sure to leave the snakes alone this time, or, according to Hyginus, trampled on them. As a result, Tiresias was released from his sentence and permitted to regain his masculinity. This ancient story is recorded in lost lines of Hesiod.

In Hellenistic and Roman times Tiresias' sex-change was embroidered upon and expanded into seven episodes, with appropriate amours in each, probably written by the Alexandrian Ptolemaeus Chennus, but attributed by Eustathius to Sostratus of Phanagoria's lost elegiac Tiresias. Tiresias is presented as a complexly liminal figure, with a foot in each of many oppositions, mediating between the gods and mankind, male and female, blind and seeing, present and future, and this world and the Underworld. According to the mythographic compendium Bibliotheke, different stories were told of the cause of his blindness, the most direct being that he was simply blinded by the gods for revealing their secrets. An alternate story told by the poet Pherecydes was followed in Callimachus' poem "The Bathing of Pallas"; in it, Tiresias was blinded by Athena after he stumbled onto her bathing naked. His mother, Chariclo, a nymph of Athena, begged Athena to undo her curse, but the goddess could not; instead, she cleaned his ears, giving him the ability to understand birdsong, thus the gift of augury. In a separate episode, Tiresias was drawn into an argument between Hera and her husband Zeus, on the theme of who has more pleasure in sex: the man, as Hera claimed; or, as Zeus claimed, the woman, as Tiresias had experienced both. Tiresias replied, "Of ten parts a man enjoys one only." Hera instantly struck him blind for his impiety. Zeus could do nothing to stop her or reverse her curse, but in recompense he did give Tiresias the gift of foresight and a lifespan of seven lives."

7. Rivers, for Morrison, symbolize both the sacred and the profane as does his use of other bodies of water (e.g. lakes, oceans, streams etc.). The use of rivers in his poetry is common and he imbues them with symbolism and mythological reference. In this instance (The *NC*, VII) the river is 'choked' which indicates that it is a symbol of life (and death) in this instance. A further extension of meaning in this regard is that the river also symbolizes humanity and that we are being slowly killed by our ideologies and faddish political manifestoes because we are losing sight of 'the way' – the mystical and sacred natural life. In the greater context of the rest of this poem (titles I-VIII), the river Nile is referenced in the first verse and in the end section, after the numbered poems (I-VIII) and before the final two number-titled poems, Morrison directly suggests that the poems, or 'catalog of Horrors,' are a '[l]ist of things in the sacred river.'

8. It is an interesting point that a predominant motif in Morrison's poetry is that of the insect. In relation to the 'cut-up' method, the insect takes on new meaning in Morrison's poems and provides a possible reason for his continual use of this motif. The etymology of the insect as given by Douglas Harper & Dan McCormack in the 'Online Etymological Dictionary' (Nov 2001) outlines the etymology of the insect as thus: "*The word "insect" comes from the Latin word insectum, meaning "with a notched or divided body", or literally "cut into", from the neuter singular past participle of insectare, "to cut into, to cut up", from in- "into" and secare "to cut"; because insects appear "cut into" three sections. Pliny the Elder introduced the Latin designation as a loan-translation of the Greek word ἔντομος (éntomos) or "insect" (as in entomology), which was Aristotle's term for this class of life, also in reference to their "notched" bodies. "Insect" first appears documented in English in 1601 in Holland's translation of Pliny. Translations of Aristotle's term also form the usual word for "insect" in Welsh (trychfil, from trychu "to cut" and mil, "animal"), Serbo-Croatian (zareznik, from rezati, "to cut"), Russian (насекомое nasekomoje, from seč'/-sekat', "to cut"), etc.*"- http://en.wikipedia.org/wiki/Insect
9. Robert Duncan, in *Stony Brook* 1—2 (Fall, 1968), p. 18.
10. Sugerman (1988), p. 188

V. Shamanism, Ideals, & Ritual

1. Aldous Huxley (Middlesex: Penguin Books, 1959). Originally published as two seperate essays (1954, 1956).
2. Lisciandro, Frank. *Jim Morrison: An Hour For Magic* (A Photo Journal) (London: A Delilah Book, Eel Pie Publishing, 1982, pg. 30)
3. *Shamanism: Archaic Techniques of Ecstasy*, translated: W.R. Trask (London: Routledge and Kegan Paul, 1964). Originally published as *Le Chamanisme*, 1951.
4. Mircea Eliade, *Shamanism, Archaic Techniques of Ecstasy*, Bollingen Series LXXVI, Princeton University Press 1972, pp. 3–7.
5. Sugerman (1988), p. 74.
6. **Deep image** is a term coined by U.S. poets Jerome Rothenberg and Robert Kelly in the second issue of the magazine *Trobar* in 1961. In general, deep image poems are resonant, stylized and heroic in tone. Longer poems tend to be catalogues of free-standing images.
7. Sherman Paul, *In Search of the Primitive* (1986), p. 178-9.
8. Paul Hoover, *Postmodern American Poetry* (1994), p. 222.
9. Baudelaire (1995), p.145.
10. Rimbaud (1966), p. 307.
11. Sugerman, *The Illustrated History of The Doors* (1988) p. 124

12. Tobler & Doe (1988), p. 48.
13. Sugerman (1988), p. 123

VI. The Influence of Style

1. John Tytell, *The Living Theatre, Art, Exile, and Outrage* (1995), pp. 256-7.
2. *Ibid.*, p. 257.
3. Antonin Artaud, *Antonin Artaud: Collected Works, Volume Four* (1974), p.64—67.
4. Tobler & Doe (1988), p. 63.
5. Artaud, *Antonin Artaud: Collected Works, Volume One* (1968), p.195.
6. Sugerman (1988), p. 67.
7. William Blake, *The Works of William Blake* (1994), p. 184.
8. Sugerman (1988), p. 123
9. See *Fifteen Poets: from Chaucer to Arnold* (1951), p. 200.
10. Hart Crane, *Complete Poems of Hart Crane* (1993), p. 8.

VII. Conclusions

1. Friedrich Nietzsche, *Beyond Good and Evil* (1917), p.9.
2. Harold Bloom, *The Western Canon: The Books and School of the Ages.* (Houghton Mifflin Harcourt, 2014), pg. 4
3. 'Wild Child: Jim Morrison's Poetic Journeys' by Tony Magistrale: (*Journal of Popular Culture*, Volume 26, Issue3, Winter 1992, Pp. 133-144) - http://onlinelibrary.wiley.com/doi/10.1111/j.0022-3840.1992.2603_133.x/abstract
4. Michael McClure, 2004. https://archives.waiting-forthe-sun.net/Pages/Legacy/Poetry/McClure.html

Bibliography

§ Primary Sources: Publications by Jim Morrison

The Lords and The New Creatures: The Only Published Poetry of Jim Morrison (London: Omnibus Press, 1985).

Wilderness: The Lost Writings of Jim Morrison (London: Penguin Group, 1990).

The American Night: The Writings of Jim Morrison (Great Britain: Viking, 1991).

§ Secondary Sources

Artaud, Antonin, *Antonin Artaud: Collected Works, Volume One*, trans. Victor Corti (London: Calder & Boyars, 1956).

Baudelaire, Charles, *Baudelaire: Selected Poems*, trans. C. Clark (London: Penguin Books Ltd., 1995).

Bibliography

Blake, William, *The Works of William Blake* (Hertfordshire: Wordsworth Editions Ltd, 1994).

Campbell, Joseph. *The Hero with a Thousand Faces* (Princeton: Princeton University Press, 1968).
— *The Masks of God, vol. 4: Creative Mythology* (New York: Viking, 1965).

Crane, Hart, *Complete Poems of Hart Crane*, ed. Marc Simon (New York: Liveright, 1993).

Davies, Douglas J., *Death, Ritual, & Belief* (London: Cassell, 1997).

Densmore, John, *Riders on the Storm: My Life With Jim Morrison & the Doors* (London: Arrow Books Limited, 1990).

Doe, Andrew & John Tobler, *In Their Own Words: The Doors* (Essex: Omnibus Press, 1988).

Douglas, John & Mark Olshaker, *Mind Hunter* (London: William Heinemann Ltd., 1995).

Duncan, Robert, in *Stony Brook* 1-2 (Fall 1968).

Fowlie, Wallace, *Rimbaud & Jim Morrison: The Rebel as Poet* (Durham: Duke University Press, 1993).
— *Rimbaud: The Myth of Childhood* (London: Dennis Dobson LTD, 1946).

Bibliography

Frazer, Sir James, *The Golden Bough: A Study in Magic & Religion* (Hertfordshire: Wordsworth Editions Ltd, 1993).

Grundlehner, Philip, *The poetry of Friedrich Nietzsche* (New York: Oxford University Press, Inc., 1986).

Hoover, Paul, ed. *Postmodern American Poetry: A Norton Anthology* (Chicago: Columbia College, 1994).

Hopkins, Jerry and Danny Sugerman, *No One Here Gets Out Alive* (Australia: Angus & Robertson, 1996).

Lisciandro, Frank, *Jim Morrison: An Hour For Magic* (A Photo Journal) (London: A Delilah Book, Eel Pie Publishing, 1982).

Manzarek, Ray, *Light My Fire: My Life with the Doors* (London: Century, 1998).

Nietzsche, Friedrich, *Daybreak: Thoughts on the Prejudices of Morality*, trans. R.J. Hollingdale (Cambridge: Cambridge University Press, 1997).
— *Beyond Good and Evil*, trans. H. Zimmern (New York: Boni & Liveright, 1917).
— *The Birth of Tragedy* (Cambridge: Cambridge University Press, 1999).
— *Thus Spake Zarathustra*, trans. Thomas Common, 1891
(http://www.eserver.org/philosophy/nietzsche-zarathustra.txt).

Bibliography

Paul, Sherman, *In Search of the Primitive* (Louisiana: Louisiana State University Press, 1986).

Rimbaud, Arthur, *Rimbaud: Complete Works, Selected Letters*, trans. Wallace Fowlie (Chicago: University of Chicago Press Ltd, 1966).
— *Rimbaud: Poems*, trans. Paul Schmidt (New York: Alfred A. Knopf, 1994).

Rothenberg, Jerome & George Quasha, *America: A prophecy: A New Reading of American Poetry from Pre-Columbian Times to the Present* (New York: Vintage Books, 1974).

Superman, Danny, *The Doors: the Illustrated History* (London: Omnibus Press 1988).

Tytell, John, *The Living Theatre, Art, Exile, and Outrage* (New York: Grove Press, 1995).

Fifteen Poets: from Chaucer to Arnold, selections by various authors/critics (London: Oxford University Press, 1951).

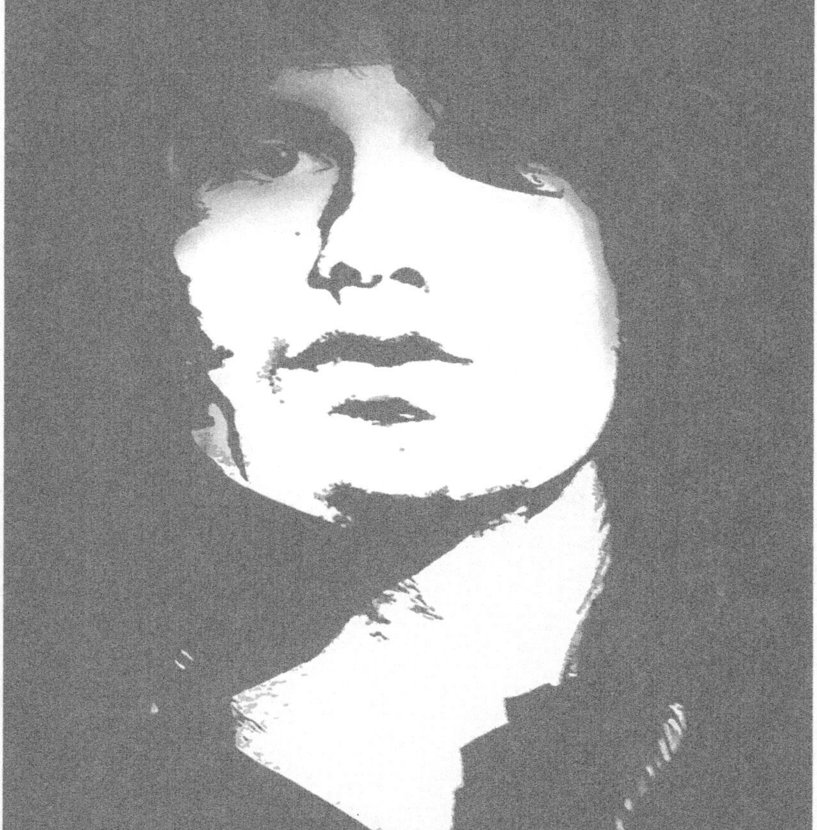

Plea to the Reader

If you enjoyed this book, please leave a review.

For other titles by William Cook and to leave a review, please visit the author's Amazon page. (Type link below into your address bar or go to www.amazon.com and search for 'William Cook gaze into the abyss')

https://www.amazon.com/William-Cook/e/B003PA513I

About the Author

William Cook was born and raised in New Zealand and is the author of the popular psychological thriller, *Blood Related*; two non-fiction books: *Gaze Into the Abyss: The Poetry of Jim Morrison* and *Secrets of Best-Selling Self-Published Authors*, and the editor of the best-selling collection *Fresh Fear: An Anthology of Macabre Horror*. William has also written many short stories that have been published in anthologies and is the author of short-fiction collections *Dark Deaths: Selected Horror Fiction*, *Babylon Fading: Bizarre Fiction & Verse*, *Serial Killer Thrillers*, and *Dreams of Thanatos*, along with two collections of poetry: *Journey: the Search for Something* and *Corpus Delicti*.

Grab a free copy of William's collection, *Dreams of Thanatos*, sign up now for the VIP newsletter at:

www.williamcookwriter.com

Also by William Cook

Novels
BLOOD RELATED

Short Fiction Collections
BABYLON FADING: Selected Bizarre Fiction & Verse
SERIAL KILLER THRILLERS V1, V2, V1 & V2
DARK DEATHS: Selected Horror Fiction
DREAMS OF THANATOS: Collected Macabre Tales

Poetry
CORPUS DELICTI: Selected Poetry

Non-Fiction
GAZE INTO THE ABYSS: The Poetry of Jim Morrison
SECRETS OF BEST-SELLING SELF-PUBLISHED AUTHORS

Edited By
FRESH FEAR: An Anthology of Macabre Horror

Printed in Great Britain
by Amazon